G. T. EMERY

17 APR 1984

45°
83

Perhaps the last photo taken of Emmy Noether, Bryn Mawr, April, 1935.

Emmy Noether
1882-1935

Auguste Dick

Translated by H. I. Blocher

1981

Birkhäuser
Boston • Basel • Stuttgart

AUGUSTE DICK
Marxergasse 18/6
A-1030 Wien
Austria

Library of Congress Cataloging in Publication Data

Dick, Auguste.
　Emmy Noether, 1882-1935.

　　Bibliography: p.
　　1.　Noether, Emmy, 1882-1935.　I.　Title.
QA29.N6D513　512'.0092'4 [B]　80-18404
ISBN 3-7643-3019-8

CIP-Kurztitelaufnahme der Deutschen Bibliothek

Dick, Auguste:
Emmy Noether : 1882-1935 / Auguste Dick.
Transl. by Heidi Blocher.-Boston, Basel,
Stuttgart : Birkhäuser, 1980.
　　Einheitssacht.: Emmy Noether <engl.>
　　ISBN 3-7643-3019-8

© Birkhäuser Boston, 1981
ISBN 3-7643-3019-8
Printed in USA

Contents

Acknowledgments

*T*HE *INCENTIVE* for examining and describing the life and work of Emmy Noether was received from a lecture by Dr. Edmund Hlawka, Professor at the University in Vienna, on the subject of the development of mathematics in the last hundred years.

Besides the books, newspapers, and magazines mentioned in the text, common reference books—in particular, Poggendorff's *Biographisch-literarisches Handwörterbuch der exakten Naturwissenschaften*—were used; in addition, mathematical journals, among them *Mathematische Annalen, Jahresberichte der Deutschen Mathematiker-Vereinigung, Journal für die reine und angewandte Mathematik, Nachrichten von der Gesellschaft der Wissenschaften zu Göttingen, Scripta mathematica, Mathematische Zeitschrift,* and others; also, *Mathematisches Wörterbuch* (Berlin-Stuttgart 1961), F. Le Lionnais, *Les grands courants de la pensée mathématique* (Paris 1962), E. T. Bell,

The Development of Mathematics, 2nd ed. (New York-London 1945), D. Hilbert, *Gesammelte Abhandlungen* (Berlin 1935), and J. R. Newman, *The World of Mathematics* (New York 1956).

Valuable information was received from the following registries and public agencies: Stadtarchive Erlangen and Mannheim; Staatsarchiv Nürnberg; Universitätsarchive Freiburg i. Br., Göttingen, and Heidelberg; Badisches Generallandesarchiv in Karlsruhe; Handschriftensammlung der Bibliothek der Eidgenössischen Technischen Hochschule, Zürich; Bayerisches Staatsministerium des Innern, Munich; Personenstandsarchiv Brühl/Köln, Amtsgericht Mannheim, Einwohnerämter of Erlangen and Göttingen, Standesämter of Berlin-Wilmersdorf, Brühl/Köln, Garzweiler, Köln, Mannheim and Wiesbaden. I also consulted the archives of Rabbi Dr. Bernhard Brilling in Münster. I wish to thank all persons involved for their valuable and sympathetic assistance. I am particularly indebted to the curator of the University of Göttingen for information from the personnel file of Prof. Dr. E. Noether, and finally to IBM, New York, for making the mural "Men of Modern Mathematics" available to me.

Oral and written information was generously contributed by Frau Prof. Elisabeth Fischer, Köln; Frau Dr. Grete Henry-

Hermann, Bremen; Frau Geheimrat Anna Pirson, Erlangen; Frau Ober-Med. Rat Dr. Charlotte Radun, Landau; Dr. Ruth Stauffer McKee, Harrisburg, Pa; Prof. Olga Taussky Todd, Pasadena; Prof. Max Deuring, Göttingen; Prof. Karl Dörge, Köln; Prof. Heinrich Grell, Berlin; Prof. Helmut Hasse, em., Hamburg; Prof. Otto Haupt, em., Erlangen; Prof. Ernst Holder, Mainz; Prof. Nathan Jacobson, New Haven, Conn.; Prof. Erich Kähler, Hamburg; Prof. Gottfried Köthe, Frankfurt am Main; Prof. Wolfgang Krull, Bonn; Prof. Karl Mayrhofer, Vienna; Prof. Georg Nöbeling, Erlangen; Prof. Gottfried Noether, Boston; Prof. Alexander Ostrowski, em., Basel; Prof. Carl Ludwig Siegel, em., Göttingen; Prof. Bartel Leendert van der Waerden, Zürich; Prof. Heinrich Kapferer, Freiburg i. Br., and Prof. Fritz Seidelmann, Munich. Mr. Clark H. Kimberling, Maryville, Missouri, furnished some details obtained in the United States.

I am deeply grateful to all these people, as well as to others not mentioned here, who have contributed to this portrait of Emmy Noether. I am especially indebted to E. Fischer and O. Todd, K. Dörge, H. Hasse, G. Noether and B. L. van der Waerden for the time and effort they have given to this project. An important source was letters in the possession of E. Fischer, O. Todd, K. Dörge, H. Hasse, and G. Noether. I wish to thank them warmly for allowing me to inspect the originals or for providing me with copies, and giving me permission to publish excerpts. I am also grateful to the staff of the library of the Eidgenössische Technische Hochschule in Zürich for permitting a partial facsimile reproduction of one of Emmy Noether's handwritten letters from their collection of manuscripts. The portrait facing page 59 is a reproduction of a photograph taken by and kindly shared by Helmut Hasse.

My warmest thanks go to Professor van der Waerden for reading the manuscript, pointing out a few defects, and kindly assisting me in correcting them. My hope is that this brief biography will offer an accurate picture and objective understanding of a great mathematician, especially for those who did not have the privilege of knowing her personally.

Vienna, November 17, 1968   A.D.

For the English translation

Over the years, Professor Olga Taussky Todd has repeatedly urged me to make my biography of Emmy Noether available to readers of English. The present volume is appearing largely as a result of Professor Taussky's encouragement and continued interest, and I thank her most sincerely.

Thanks are also due to Dr. Bernhard Roider for his assistance in proofreading the English translation, and to the publisher for making the English edition of my book such an attractive volume.

This edition incorporates a few additions to the original text. Moreover, when I was able to update my original information, as in recording the deaths of colleagues, I have done so. As when the Japanese edition was published in 1975, I am very happy to have this opportunity to share with an even wider audience Emmy Noether's incomparable personality and the remarkable story of her life.

Vienna, August 1980   A.D.

Chronology

1882 March 23. Emmy Noether born in Erlangen

1900 April. Bavarian examinations for female teachers of French and English, in Ansbach

1903 July 14. *Reifeprüfung**, Königliches Realgymnasium, Nuremberg

1907 December 13. Doctor's degree (Dr. phil.) in Erlangen

1915 April. Moved to Göttingen

1915 May 9. Mother dies in Erlangen

1919 June 4. *Habilitation** in Göttingen

1921 December 13. Father dies in Erlangen

1922 April 6. Named *"ausserordentlicher Professor"**

1923 Summer. Teaching assignment in algebra

1925 August. Completion of manuscript, "Abstrakter Aufbau der Idealtheorie in Zahl- und Funktionenkörpern"

* See Appendix C for explanation of ranks and academic terms.

1928 September 5. Communication to the International Congress of Mathematics in Bologna, "Hyperkomplexe Grössen und Darstellungstheorie in arithmetischer Auffassung," Internationaler Mathematiker— Kongress, Bologna

1928–1929 Visiting professor in Moscow

1930 Visiting professor in Frankfurt/Main

1932 June 1. Completion of the manuscript, "Nichtkommutative Algebren"

1932 Ackermann-Teubner Gedächtnispreis (memorial award)

1932 September 7. Lecture, "Hyperkomplexe Grössen und ihre Beziehungen zur kommutativen Algebra und zur Zahlentheorie," Internationaler Mathematiker-Kongress, Zurich

1933 April. Withdrawal of permission to teach, with reference to § 3 of the law "zur Wiederherstellung des Berufsbeamtentums"

1933 October. Aboard the "Bremen," to become visiting professor in the United States

1934 Last publication, "Zerfallende verschränkte Produkte und ihre Maximalordnungen. Von Emmy Noether in Göttingen z. Zt. Bryn Mawr, Penna"

1934 Trip to Germany; final emigration to the USA

1935 April 7. Last letter to Helmut Hasse

1935 April 14. Unexpected death following an operation in Bryn Mawr, PA, USA

Introduction

*I*N *1964* at the World's Fair in New York City one room was dedicated solely to mathematics. The display included a very attractive and informative mural, about 13 feet long, sponsored by one of the largest computer manufacturing companies and presenting a brief survey of the history of mathematics. Entitled, "Men of Modern Mathematics," it gives an outline of the development of that science from approximately 1000 B.C. to the year of the exhibition. The first centuries of this time span are illustrated by pictures from the history of art and, in particular, architecture; the period since 1500 is illuminated by portraits of mathematicians, including brief descriptions of their lives and professional achievements. Close to eighty portraits are crowded into a space of about fourteen square feet; among them, only one is of a woman. Her face—mature, intelligent, neither pretty nor handsome—may suggest her love of science and creative gift, but certainly reveals a likeable personality and a genuine kindness of heart. It is the portrait of Emmy Noether (1882–1935), surrounded by the likenesses of such famous men as Joseph Liouville (1809–1882), Georg Cantor (1845–1918), and David Hilbert (1862–1943). It is accompanied by the following text:

> Emmy Noether, daughter of the mathematician Max, was often called "Der Noether," as if she were a man. Yet her Göttingen professorship carried no salary, and Hilbert had to fight to get her—a woman—in at all. She was fat, rough, and loud, but so kind, humorous and sociable that all who knew her loved her. With the Nazi rise to power she left for the United States.
>
> Emmy's early work on invariants gave no hint that she would become one of the creators of abstract axiomatic algebra. She developed the axiomatic theory of ideals, introducing the ascending chain condition; gave a unified theory of non-commutative algebras and their representations; defined the "verschränktes Produkt" and, with Brauer and Hasse, proved that every simple algebra over an algebraic number field is cyclic.

To give an idea of the degree of importance represented by the mathematicians chosen for this display, we only need to quote the last group of names (arranged by year of death): N. Wiener (1894–1964), T. Skolem

(1887–1963), W. Blaschke (1885–1962), E. Artin (1898–1962), C. de la Vallée–Poussin (1866–1962), J. Hadamard (1865–1962), O. Veblen (1880–1960), J. H. C. Whitehead (1904–1960), T. Takagi (1875–1960), E. Cartan (1869–1951), G Hardy (1877–1947), G. D. Birkhoff (1884–1944), H. Lebesgue (1875–1941), E. Lasker (1868–1941). A number of these men were working in the same field as Emmy Noether, or one closely related; among them, Takagi, the Japanese representative of algebraic number theory (and one of the people who testified on Emmy Noether's behalf in order to prevent her dismissal by the Nazi authorities), and Emanuel Lasker, popularly known as world chess champion, who was the first to prove that every polynomial ideal is an intersection of primary ideals. (The DDR honored him as "Significant Personality" by issuing a postage stamp with his portrait.) Emil Artin was one of E. Noether's more intimate friends; it was in his Institute in Hamburg that, on her final trip from her North American exile to her still cherished Göttingen in June 1934, she delivered—as an "invited foreign guest"—her inspired and inspiring lectures on her newest insights in the field of noncommutative algebras.

The Erlangen Period

(1882–1915)

*A*MALIE EMMY NOETHER was born—the first child of Jewish parents—on March 23, 1882 in Erlangen in Southern Germany. Since 1743 this provincial town, Bavarian since 1810, had one of the three existing "free" universities (i.e., a university founded independent of the churches)—the other two being in Halle (since 1697) and in Göttingen (since 1737). The first outstanding mathematician at the University of Erlangen was Christian von Staudt (1798–1867), whose work is fundamental to synthetic geometry. But it was Felix Klein (1849–1925) who brought world fame in mathematics to Erlangen with his inaugural lecture of 1872, explaining the significance, first recognized by him, of the concept of a group in geometry. His insights became known as the "Erlangen Program" and doubtless are the reason why Erlangen is the town most frequently mentioned in mathematical litera-

4

ture. One of Felix Klein's friends and colleagues, Paul Gordan (1837–1912), was a colleague of Max Noether (1844–1921), whose daughter was to become Gordan's only female doctoral candidate—something that would have been beyond anyone's imagination at the time of her birth. Girls were not destined for the study of science, least of all mathematics. Yet, this little Jewish girl not only became a mathematician but was to become one of the most important creators in the field of abstract algebra.

Emmy's father, Max Noether, was born in 1844 in Mannheim and died in 1921 in Erlangen. He was the descendant of a line of wealthy wholesale dealers of hardware. His grandfather, Elias Samuel (1774?–1846), the eldest of at least six brothers, left Bühl in the northern Black Forest in approximately 1797 and moved to Bruchsal, where he founded a business and a family. At that time Bruchsal was still the property of the Archbishops of Speyer and offered more favorable conditions for Jews than other towns along the Rhine. At the beginning of the nineteenth century Bruchsal, as part of the Palatinate on the right side of the Rhine, was included in the Grand Duchy of Baden which was just being formed. In 1809, the Tolerance Edict of Baden stated that the male head of every Jewish family who did not already have a distinguishing hereditary surname was to assume one for himself and his children. Elias Samuel, along with his wife and their nine children, was given the name Nöther. This could be traced back for centuries as a non-Jewish family name. Elias Samuel's youngest brother Raphael, who resided in Gernsbach, also called himself Nöther, while the four brothers remaining in Bühl—Hertz, Wolf, Jakob and Isaak—as well as their father, bore the name Netter, which probably existed prior to the edict. Presumably, Netter was derived from Nathan, which would explain why this name is so common in the area of Strasbourg (about 40 miles southwest of Bühl). Not all Netters (and there are many distinguished persons among them, especially in the French–speaking area) are related to the Noethers, but those in the hardware business are likely to be. Elias Samuel's grandson Max, the mathematician, and his children used the spelling Noether, although Max's marriage documents still show the official spelling as Nöther. Along with the adoption of a family name came the Christianization of first names. Thus, Hertz, son of Elias Samuel, became Hermann Nöther. Hermann was the first in the family to take up academic studies, whether by his own inclination or the wish of his parents. At any rate, he left his hometown Bruchsal at the age of eighteen to study theology at the Lemle–Moses–Stiftung—also called the

Klaus School—in Mannheim. He abandoned this course later on, however, and became a merchant instead. In 1837, together with one of his older brothers, he founded the firm of Joseph Nöther & Co. in Mannheim, a wholesale hardware business, which eventually branched out to Düsseldorf and Berlin and at last fell sacrifice to "Aryanization", after existing for a century.

Hermann's wife, Amalia Würzburger from Mannheim—who also appears as Malche and Malchen in the documents—bore five children. The middle one, Max, became the mathematician. It was assumed in the family later on that his mathematical talent came from his mother's side. Max was the first of the Noethers to become a doctor of philosophy. In the following generations there were a considerable number, with at least three mathematicians and three chemists among them. Several of them, like Max, became university professors. One of Max's many cousins, Ferdinand Nöther (1834–1918) studied medicine in Heidelberg and practiced in Mannheim from 1870 on. All the other males became merchants. In the following generation, however, there was a painter, a certified engineer, and a writer.

Max Noether had the misfortune of being stricken with polio at the age of fourteen, after which he was lame for the rest of his life. In 1880, as a mature man in the position of a Royal Bavarian ausserordentlicher Universitätsprofessor* he married Ida Amalia Kaufmann (1852, Cologne—1915, Erlangen) in Wiesbaden, daughter of a very wealthy Jewish family whose ancestors on both sides had been settled in the Lower Rhine area for generations, while Max Noether's ancestors came from the Black Forest region and Mannheim.

The Kaufmanns, sons of cattle dealers and butchers from the purely agricultural regions west of Cologne, became wholesale merchants in that city, owning property in the neighboring areas. Markus Kaufmann (1813, Garzweiler—1866, Brühl near Cologne) married Friederike Scheuer, a banker's daughter from Düsseldorf whose ancestors on her father's side had been rabbis for several generations; her family tree supposedly can be traced back to 1533. Markus Kaufmann and Friederike Scheuer had ten other children besides Ida. One of them, Wilhelm (1858, Cologne—1926, Berlin) became a university professor in Berlin and a well-known specialist in questions of finance and economics as they pertain to international law. He and his brother Paul, a wholesaler in Berlin, accumulated part of the small fortune which later sustained Emmy Noether.

* *ausserordentlicher:* with somewhat limited administrative functions

Emmy had two slightly younger brothers born in 1883 and 1884, with whom she spent her early childhood in their parents' home in Erlangen. In 1889 another brother was born. For about 45 years the Noethers were tenants of the same large second-floor apartment in an ugly apartment house at 30–32 Nürnberger Strasse. Incidentally, Prof. Eilhard Wiedemann, a physicist and specialist in Islamic culture, lived in the same building with his family, also for a very long time. The story is that they used up so much of the common water supply that Frau Noether felt at a disadvantage since both families shared the expense equally.

Emmy did not appear exceptional as a child. Playing among her peers in the schoolyard on Fahrstrasse she probably was not especially noticeable—a near-sighted, plain-looking little girl, though not without charm. Her teachers and classmates knew Emmy as a clever, friendly, and likeable child. She had a slight lisp and was one of the few who attended classes in the Jewish religion.

The following little anecdote, however, may show how Emmy did excel among her peers. A professor's daughter remembers, seventy years later, how at a children's party Emmy attracted attention by her unusual quickness of mind. The children were being entertained with various guessing games, and were posed a rather complex question—of the kind that in mathematics is known as a "combination problem." Before the other children, who looked rather puzzled, had even begun to rack their young brains for the answer, Emmy burst out, "But of course, the answer is so and so," and immediately produced the correct solution.

From 1889 to 1897 Emmy's name appears in the class lists of the Städtische Höhere Töchterschule (Municipal School for Higher Education of Daughters) in Erlangen, first as Emmy, later as Emma Noether. At that time this school was located at 35 Friedrichstrasse in the former Lyncker Palace which had been built, along with other aristocratic mansions, in the early 18th century, after Erlangen had become Residenzstadt (the monarch's residence) in 1708. Judging by the curricula preserved in the archives of the town of Erlangen, the material taught at this school was very similar to that offered at institutions for higher education today at the junior level (without Latin). Possibly the level of German, French, and mathematics went somewhat higher. As was customary at that time for girls receiving a higher education (called "Höhere Töchter"—higher daughters), Emmy also had piano lessons, but it is said that she never went beyond "Der fröhliche Landmann" (The Happy Farmer, a popular piece for beginners)—

quite in contrast to her mother who, almost up to the time of her death, devotedly practiced *"Hausmusik"* with an excellent violinist. It seems that Emmy also took part in household activities, although probably without much fervor, and clearly without being permanently affected. The amusing stories her students told later of her own housekeeping in Göttingen do not imply thorough training in domestic work, or much talent for it. She was more successful in the study of French and English, with which she occupied herself after her school years were over. One of her favorite recreational activities was dancing; even today they tell stories in Erlangen of how Emmy used to look forward to dances in the homes of professors, and how parents admonished their sons to be sure to ask Emmy Noether to dance. Many a young man might have preferred a prettier partner or a more graceful dancer. And mathematics, after all, was not yet the topic of brilliant conversation with her that it would later become.

In the spring of 1900 Miss Noether, now eighteen, registered in Ansbach for the examinations required by the state of Bavaria for teachers of French and English. The examinations were held from April 2 to 6. The evaluation scale included twelve grades, 1 being the highest. Emmy Noether achieved an average of 1.2 in each language, which produced the overall grade "very good" ("sehr gut"). It is characteristic of her that only in "classroom teaching" did she fall below this grade—to 2. Even later, as a university lecturer, she would not have done better.

Passing these examinations entitled her to teach modern languages at "institutions for the education and instruction of females" ("weibliche Erziehungs- und Unterrichtsanstalten"). But instead she thought of continuing her studies at the university level. At that time in Germany, only very few women attended university lectures. Emmy Noether became one of them. Most were certified teachers who listed "continued education" as the purpose of their studies. They were not allowed to enroll as regular students but were only admitted as auditors without access to examinations, and only if the professor whose lectures they wished to attend gave permission. Not infrequently, permission was withheld, and even after this policy of discrimination had been abandoned, one professor in Berlin refused to begin his lecture if a woman was present in the room. As late as 1908 the Prussian Ministry of Education found it necessary to state that women's access to lectures "must not be determined by the degree of the individual lecturer's distaste for co-education." In the lists for the winter semester of 1900/01 in Erlangen two female auditors are registered—that is, one besides Emmy Noether—as compared with 984 male students. An impression of what women studying at a university were confronted with at the beginning of the twentieth century particularly in mathematics, is given by Gerhard Kowalewski (1876–1950) in his book "Bestand und Wandel" (Continuation and Change) (Munich, 1950).

It is interesting to note that in the curriculum vitae attached to Emmy Noether's doctoral dissertation, a professor in Roman studies, Julius Pirson (1870–1959), and a historian, Richard Fester (1860–1945), are mentioned as her teachers at the University of Erlangen. Does this indicate that she was hesitating at first between mathematics and modern languages? At any rate, while auditing at the university in her home town between 1900 and 1902, she was at the same time preparing for the *Reifeprüfung** (graduation exams) which she took on July 14, 1903 at the *Königliches Realgymnasium*** (Royal College for semiclassical education) in Nuremberg. This school, called Willstätter-Gymnasium after 1945, had a very good reputation. Richard Willstätter (1872–1942), who received the Nobel prize for chemistry in

* *Reifeprüfung:* a graduation exam usually taken at age 19 entitling the graduate to enter a university of his choice
** *Realgymnasium:* a type of high school, with emphasis on the sciences, mathematics, and modern languages

1915, was a student there for six years, from *Untertertia** to graduation; in his autobiography "Aus meinem Leben" (From My Life—Weinheim 1949) he speaks of his teachers and the chairman of the board of examiners, Aurel Voss (1845–1931), a mathematician, with affection and gratitude. This same man might have examined Emmy Noether; we do not know since all documents concerning the *Realgymnasium* in Nuremberg were lost in World War II.

After graduation Emmy spent her first semester at the University in Göttingen, where she is listed as *Hospitant* (auditor) for the winter semester 1903–04. From her curriculum vitae we know that she attended lectures by the astronomer Karl Schwarzschild (1873–1916) and the mathematicians Hermann Minkowski (1864–1909), Otto Blumenthal (1876–1944), Felix Klein, and David Hilbert. After the first semester she returned to Erlangen. At this point the law was changed to allow female university students to enroll properly and take examinations with the same rights as their male peers. On October 24, 1904, Emmy Noether matriculated at the University of Erlangen as number 468. At that time she only listed mathematics as her course of study. Thus she belonged to Section II of the school of philosophy, which

* *Untertertia:* eighth grade

included an enrolled student body of 46 males and 1 female. The only other faculty besides philosophy women were choosing at that time was medicine. These two faculties included 205 students in the year of Emmy Noether's enrollment, among them two female auditors and four "matriculated ladies."

In the meantime, two of Emmy's brothers also had entered the university. Alfred, Emmy's junior by one year, was studying chemistry, entirely in Erlangen except for the winter semester 1904/05 which he spent in Freiburg. He received his doctorate in 1909. In 1918 he died in Erlangen, possibly because his weak constitution could not endure the deprivations of the last years of the war. Emmy's second brother, Fritz, born on October 7, 1884 in Erlangen, studied mathematics and physics in Erlangen and Munich. He obtained his doctor's degree under Aurel Voss in Munich, where he also worked with Sommerfeld (1868–1951). Later, although he served in the army during the war, his career advanced quickly at the colleges for higher technology (Technische Hochschulen) in Karlsruhe and Breslau. There were semesters when no fewer than three of the Noether children daily made their way from Nürnbergerstrasse to the University, where Fritz and Emmy also attended their father's lectures. Max Noether had become *Or-*

*dinarius** in Erlangen years before and was responsible, along with Paul Gordan, seven years his senior, for the main courses.

Hans Falckenberg (1885–1946), also a professor's son, was a close friend of the Noether children. He and Fritz Noether served in the army together, both during their student years. After a few semesters of studying law, Falckenberg, too, switched to mathematics. Emmy Noether referred to him in 1919 as her first doctoral candidate. He himself wrote in 1911 that he was deeply indebted to both Max and Emmy Noether, to Emmy especially for leaving to him the subject of his thesis (which she had been considering for her own research) and for assisting him in so many ways in writing it. He later became *ordentlicher Universitätsprofessor*** of mathematics at the University of Giessen.

Under Gordan's influence Emmy Noether wrote a paper based on the theory of invariants, entitled, On the construction of the system of forms for the ternary biquadratic form ("Über die Bildung des Formensystems der ternären biquadratischen Form"). It was registered as her doctoral dissertation in the *Erlanger Universitätsschriften* 1907/08 number 202, dated July 2, 1908. Before its first complete printing, an excerpt of it appeared, with

* *Ordinarius:* full professor.
** *ordentlicher Universitätsprofessor:* full professor.

the same title, in the conference reports of the Physikalisch-medizinische Sozietät (Society for Physics and Medicine) in Erlangen (#39, 1907, pp. 176–179). This excerpt seems to have been Emmy Noether's first publication. The whole of her thesis was printed in the *Journal für die reine und angewandte Mathematik*, 134, 1908, pp. 23–90; it ends with a large table of more than 300 explicitly stated invariants. The *Erlanger Universitätsschrift* is a repaginated special reprint of the journal article. The subject of this dissertation as well as its treatment correspond entirely to Gordan's interest. They do not indicate in any way the course that the author's thinking later took toward purely abstract algebra. Emmy Noether herself later referred to her thesis, as well as to several consecutive papers on the theory of invariants, as "crap." In 1932 she declared that as far as she was concerned, her dissertation was forgotten; in fact she couldn't even remember in which volume of Crelle's journal it had been published. Once Karl Petri (1881–1955), a former *Assistent** in Erlangen who had joined the public school service (as a teacher) but continued to do scientific work and remained in close contact with the Noether family, asked Emmy to read a manuscript of his. It

---

* *Assistent:* assistant professor

was along the line of her own dissertation, and since Emmy had edited papers by Petri before, she seemed the logical person to do it. Instead, she confessed, "I have completely forgotten all of the symbolic calculation I ever learned," and proceeded to look for another reviewer for Petri's work. Another time, when she pronounced a very harsh judgement on a dissertation which had been accepted by a well-respected professor, she was made to endure the humiliation of being reminded of her own thesis.

Emmy Noether passed the oral examination required for the degree of doctor of philosophy on Friday, December 13, 1907, with the distinction of summa cum laude. During the following years she worked—without salary or commission—at the Mathematical Institute in Erlangen, partly in order to relieve her aging and increasingly disabled father, partly on her own projects, still involved with algebraic invariants. Apparently, by this time it had become clear to her that her life would be devoted to research in mathematics. In 1908 she became a member of the Circolo matematico di Palermo, and in 1909 of the Deutsche Mathematiker Vereinigung (DMV—German Association of Mathematicians). The large annual meetings of the DMV gave young mathematicians the opportunity to present the results of their re-

search, to inform themselves on new directions pursued in the field, and, occasionally,
to take a privileged look into the "workshop"
of a well-known specialist. During the discussions which usually followed the lectures,
people were able to meet each other and find
out, on an informal level, "what was doing in
mathematics." Whenever possible, these annual meetings were arranged to coincide
with the semi-annual Conference of German
Natural Scientists and Physicians (Versamm-
lung Deutscher Naturforscher und Ärzte).
Emmy Noether loved these meetings and
frequently took advantage of them to give
a lecture herself. They filled her natural
desire to be with other mathematicians, to
exchange ideas with them and become inspired, and to get plenty of opportunities,
outside of the sessions, "to talk mathematics," as she called it. In the evening, after the
official meeting, the members used to meet
for informal "after sessions." These often
lasted rather long, and were not in an
academic setting. Emmy took part and, especially in the first years of her membership,
she was often the only active female member
present—the other ladies being the wives of
mathematicians. In 1909 she already gave
her first lecture to the DMV, in Salzburg. Her
brother Fritz, who had received his doctor's
degree shortly before and had dedicated him-

self to applied mathematics, also spoke there. The following is a complete list of the lectures given by Emmy Noether at the DMV:

1909 Salzburg

Zur Invariantentheorie der Formen von n Variabeln

(On the theory of invariants for the forms of n variables)

1913 Vienna

Über rationale Funktionenkörper
(On fields of rational functions)

1920 Bad Nauheim

Fragen der Modul- und Idealtheorie
(Problems in the theory of modules and ideals)

1921 Jena

Über eine Arbeit des im Krieg gefallenen K. Hentzelt zur Eliminationstheorie
(On a paper on elimination theory by K. Hentzelt, who was killed in the war.)

1922 Leipzig

Algebraische und Differentialinvarianten (Bericht)
(Algebraic and differential invariants (a report))

1923 Marburg an der Lahn

Eliminationstheorie und Idealtheorie
(Elimination theory and the theory of ideals)

1924 Innsbruck

Abstrakter Aufbau der Idealtheorie im algebraischen Zahlkörper
(The abstract foundation of ideal theory in algebraic number fields)

1925 Danzig

Gruppencharaktere und Idealtheorie
(Group characters and ideal theory)

1929 Prague

Idealdifferentiation und Differente
(Differentiation of ideals and the different)

In addition to these, the following two lectures were given at international congresses of mathematicians:

1928 Bologna

Hyperkomplexe Grössen und Darstellungstheorie in arithmetischer Auffassung
(Mitteilung in einer Sektionssitzung)
(Hypercomplex quantities and representation theory from the arithmetical point of view) (Communication from a section meeting)

1932 Zurich

Hyperkomplexe Systeme in ihren Beziehungen zur kommutativen Algebra und zur Zahlentheorie (grosser Vortrag in einer allgemeinen Sitzung)
(Hypercomplex systems with a view to commutative algebra and to number theory) (major lecture in a general meeting)

In reference to Emmy Noether's stay in Vienna in 1913, a grandson of Franz Mertens (1840—1927) remembered, 65 years later:

One of my grandfather's mathematical acquaintances was Emmy Noether. It must have been around 1912 that she visited him at the Stammgasse. It may also be that she came to see us several times. I clearly recall a visitor who, although a woman, seemed to me like a Catholic chaplain from a rural parish—dressed in a black, almost ankle-length, and rather nondescript coat, a man's hat on her short hair (still a rarity at that time), and with a shoulder bag carried crosswise like those of the railroad conductors during the imperial period, she was a rather odd figure. She must have been in her late twenties or early thirties then. I would easily have taken her for a clergyman from one of the neighboring villages. When I questioned my grandfather about this strange visitor, he explained to me that she was a mathematician, a scholar who had come to converse with him on scientific matters.

Let us return to Erlangen. In 1910 Gordan retired from his position as *Ordinarius*. His successor, Erhard Schmidt (1876–1959), had little impact on Erlangen, although one of his papers was the incentive for Hans Falckenberg's dissertation "Verzweigungen von Lösungen nichtlinearer Differential- gleichungen" (Ramifications of solutions of nonlinear differential equations). Schmidt was followed by Ernst Fischer (1875—1954); it is he who became a true mentor to Emmy Noether. With him she could "talk mathe- matics" to her heart's desire. Although both lived in Erlangen and saw each other fre- quently at the University, a large number of postcards exist from E. Noether to E. Fischer, containing mathematical arguments. Looking over this correspondence, one gets the im- pression that immediately after a conversa- tion with Fischer Emmy Noether sat down and continued the ideas discussed in writing, whether so as not to forget them, or whether to stimulate another discussion. Ernst Fischer has succeeded in carefully preserving these communications through all the havoc of war. The correspondence extends from 1911 to 1929 and is most frequent in 1915, just before Emmy Noether moved to Göttingen and Ernst Fischer was drafted by the military. There can be no doubt that it was under Fischer's influence that Emmy Noether made the definite change from the purely computational distinctly algorithmical approach represented by Gordan to the mode of thinking characteristic of Hilbert. In addition to Ernst Fischer and Max Noether (who was now old and no longer creatively productive), there was at this time a young mathematician in Erlangen by the name of Richard Baldus (1885—1945), a student of Max Noether. However, he was drafted right at the beginning of his career in 1914. Both Emmy Noether and Ernst Fischer thought highly of him, although his interests were focused in entirely different areas.

The spring of 1915 brought Emmy Noether's move to Göttingen. In her curriculum vitae, attached to the document admitting her as a lecturer (*Habilitierungsakt*) in Göttingen in 1919, she writes, "In the summer of 1915 I came to Göttingen, following an invitation by the mathematicians here." In a letter to Helmut Hasse, dated July 21, 1933, Emmy Noether mentions that, "In a questionnaire I recently received I stated that Klein and Hilbert brought me to Göttingen in the spring of 1915 to substitute for the *Privatdozenten*.* According to the records of the offices of registration in Erlangen and Göttingen, Emmy Noether actually moved at the end of April, 1915. Exactly two weeks after her departure her mother died in Erlangen—unexpectedly,

---

* *Privatdozent:* a person who has acquired the right to teach, *venia legendi,* without being on the paid staff of the university.

Emmy Noether on a stroll in the country with Hasse and an unidentified woman.

The former Lyncker Palace in Erlangen (Friedrichstrasse 35, at the corner of Fahrstrasse). The Städtische Höhere Töchterschule, which Emmy Noether attended from 1889 through 1897, was housed in this building. (Photo 1966)

Max Noether (1844–1921)

it must be assumed, since otherwise it is unlikely that her daughter would have moved away at exactly that time. Emmy returned to stay with her aged father for several weeks, since in Ida Amalia he had lost not only his wife and the mother of his children, but also the person he had depended on for his care.

Little is known of this woman, either from written or oral accounts, yet, taking everything into consideration, official documents included, we arrive at a certain picture. She grew up in Cologne and on an estate in Brühl in a family of means; at 14 she lost her father; she had ten siblings; her youngest sister readily assisted the Noether family whenever personal help was needed; one of her brothers became a university professor; she was single and childless at the time of her engagement to Max Noether, and living with her mother in Wiesbaden; she enjoyed music and played the piano at home; as a housewife she was most frugal, almost stingy; she bore at least four children of whom Emmy and Fritz gave her much joy while Alfred and Gustav Robert caused her considerable worry because of their illnesses; a few weeks before her death she underwent medical treatment for an eye problem. It is left to us to imagine how much strength the life of this woman, and wife of a physically handicapped and otherwise difficult man, must have required. An additional detail mentioned in the obituary of Max Noether by Alexander Brill

(1842–1935) is that Frau Noether undertook several long trips with her husband, one of them to Venice where they attended Easter mass at San Marco. These are the meager facts we have concerning the mother of a woman mathematician of genius. In his book *Men of Mathematics* (New York, 1937, and Penguin, 1965), E. T. Bell (1883–1961) says that it is typically German to consider only the fathers in most biographies of prominent persons.

During frequent trips between Göttingen and Erlangen in the first years of the war, Emmy Noether was preoccupied with the old question, "is any given permutation group the Galois group of some equation?" This question was first raised by Dedekind (1831–1916) and introduced to Noether in Göttingen by Landau. She was also preoccupied with the dissertation by Seidelmann, whom she later called her second doctoral candidate. Fritz Seidelmann, from Rosenheim, had been an instructor at the Lehrerinnen-bildungsanstalt (college for women teachers) in Erlangen since the fall of 1914. While studying with Friedrich Hartogs (1874–1943) in Munich, he had produced an examination paper on equations of degree four with pre-assigned group in which he had been able to establish successfully the equations for special cases. In Erlangen he asked Max Noether whether this paper might be worked out as a dissertation. Since Emmy Noether happened to be involved with the theme "given the group, find the equation" at that time, her father referred Seidelmann to her. After she had drawn his attention to the tool of parametric representation he was then able to solve the problem generally for third and fourth-degree equations. Although Emmy was already in Göttingen at that time, she was able to assist Seidelmann with writing his thesis, during her vacations, which she spent working at her parents' house in Erlangen. The dissertation was entitled *Die Gesamtheit der kubischen und biquadratischen Gleichungen mit Affekt bei beliebigem Rationalitätsbereich* (The set of cubic and biquadratic equations with affect over an arbitrary field). It was printed in 1916 with the note, "Dedicated to Frl. Dr. Emmy Noether." Fritz Seidelmann passed his oral examination summa cum laude, a fact which, by his own account, delighted Emmy Noether as much as it did him. The *Mathematische Annalen,* vol. 78 (1917/18) published Emmy Noether's paper *"Gleichungen mit vorgeschriebener Gruppe"* (Equations with pre-assigned group), finished in Göttingen in July 1916, and up to then the most significant contribution on this problem. It was followed by an excerpt from Seidelmann's dissertation. Fifty years later Seidelmann still remembers Emmy Noether with deep reverence.

The Göttingen Period

(1915–1933)

*I*N *1893*, Hilbert traced the historical development of the theory of algebraic invariants, dividing it into three periods:
• *The naive period*, represented by the
originators of the theory of invariants, the
"invariant-twins" Cayley (1821–1895)—
from whose forehead, to quote H. Weyl
(1885–1955), "this theory sprang around
1850 not unlike Minerva from the forehead
of Jupiter, covered with the brilliant shield of
algebra"—and Sylvester (1814–1897),
whose penetrating intelligence, according to
MacMahon (1854–1929), made of it a perfect work of art, admired by generations of
mathematicians;
• *The period of symbolic calculus*, invented
by Aronhold (1819–1884) and Clebsch
(1833–1872), much applied by the latter and
his school and used with greatest virtuosity
by Gordan even in carrying out gigantic
mathematical operations, and still used by

28

Hilbert in his dissertation and several later papers;

• The third period, called by Hilbert *the "critical" period*, which he himself initiated and brought to culmination. In 1888, during Easter vacation, Hilbert went to Erlangen and Göttingen. His first visit was to Gordan, "the king of invariants," who had established and proved his theorem of finiteness (*Endlichkeitssatz*) in 1868/69: "*Jede Kovariante und Invariante einer binären Form ist eine ganze Funktion mit numerischen Koeffizienten einer endlichen Anzahl solcher Formen.*" As a result of his conversation with Gordan, Hilbert was able to solve the problem of finiteness of the system of invariants (*Endlichkeit des Invariantensystems*) on a general level, that is, for algebraic forms in n variables—not by the symbolic method, which is entirely unsuited for this operation, but by that mode of purely abstract thinking which was to characterize all of his work from then on. This proof was purely existential. Hilbert concluded his investigations of the theory of invariants in his papers, "On the theory of algebraic forms," and "On the complete systems of invariants," published in 1890 and 1893. Simultaneously, these papers contain the foundations for the theory of abstract fields, rings, and modules which was to influence Emmy Noether by way of Ernst Fischer, whose thinking was a direct continuation of Hilbert's and Mertens'

(1840–1927). In May 1914, Emmy Noether completed her manuscript "Fields and systems of rational functions" ("Körper und Systeme rationaler Funktionen"), which carries the note, "The incentive for this work was given by my conversations with Mr. Fischer . . . ". In 1915, E. Fischer writes in the *Göttinger Nachrichten,* p. 78, about research projects which Noether had already carried out a few years earlier on his instigation. And finally, in 1919, Emmy Noether states in a curriculum vitae that it was Fischer who had awakened her interest in abstract algebra, approached from the point of view of arithmetic, and that this had determined all her later work. Thus, penetrating Hilbert's previous field of interest more and more deeply, Emmy Noether at last came to be considered a specialist in the theory of invariants. That Klein and Hilbert called her to Göttingen surely was not simply because they wished to do their long-time colleague Max Noether a favor, or because they wanted to give a talented woman a chance; it was in their own interest as well that they invited her, and already in 1915, attempted to establish a lectureship for her (*Habilitierung*) although without success. In November 1915, E. Noether writes to E. Fischer, "The theory of invariants is the thing here now; even the physicist Hertz is studying Gordan-Kerschensteiner; Hilbert plans to lecture next week about his ideas on Einstein's differential invariants, and so our crowd had better be ready." At about the same time she mentioned to Seidelmann that a team in Göttingen, to which she belonged, was carrying out calculations of the most difficult kind for Einstein (1879–1955)—"although," she chuckled, "none of us understands what they are for." Felix Klein says in a letter to Hilbert, "You know that Frl. Noether is continually advising me in my projects and that it is really through her that I have become competent in the subject . . . ". Hilbert's response to this letter contains this fragment, "Emmy Noether, whom I called upon to help me with such questions as my theorem on the conservation of energy . . . ". (F. Klein presented excerpts from this correspondence, referring to a paper by Hilbert, *Grundlagen der Physik* (Fundamentals of physics), to the Gesellschaft der Wissenschaften (Society for the Sciences) in Göttingen in January 1918.) It is a fact, then, that the "expert in the theory of invariants," as Hilbert once jokingly called himself, turned to the pupil of the "king of invariants" for help!

On November 9, 1915, in an effort to obtain *Habilitation*, Emmy Noether gave a lecture before the Mathematical Society in Göttingen entitled *Über ganze transzendente Zahlen* (On transcendental integers). On this occasion she comments to Fischer, "Even our geographer came to hear it and found it rather too abstract; the faculty wants to make sure it's not going to be duped at the meeting by the mathematicians." Duped or not, the deal was never made; *Habilitation* was declared impossible because of "unmet legal requirements"! According to the *Privat-dozentenverordnung* (regulations concerning *Privatdozenten*) of 1908, *Habilitation* could only be granted to male candidates. An appeal to the Minister of Culture was rejected. Hilbert's objection (not positively authenticated but willingly repeated)—that he couldn't see why the gender of the candidate should be an argument against admission as a *Privatdozent*; after all, this was a university, not a bathing establishment—effected nothing.

In the catalogue of lectures for the winter semester 1916/17 of the Georg-August-University in Göttingen, we find the following listing: "Mathematical-physical seminar. Theory of invariants: Prof. Hilbert, with the assistance of Frl. Dr. E. Noether, Mondays 4–6 P.M., free of charge." From then on, this was a standing addition to all listings of Hilbert's seminars, problem sessions, and even main lectures, up to and including the summer semester of 1919.

In the meantime, the war had come to an end, and the changes in the political structures brought profound social transformations, including a betterment of the legal position of women. For Emmy Noether this meant the possibility of *Habilitation*. During the war years, Frl. Dr. Noether had not only "assisted" David Hilbert, that is, given lectures and taught problem sessions in his name; she also had been pursuing her own projects. In 1917 and 1918 she occupied herself with differential invariants. On August 22, 1917, she writes to Ernst Fischer, "I have actually been able now to reduce the differential invariants—which up to last spring I still had not completely proved—to a problem of equivalence between linear families; it would be nice if this could be incorporated into your theory"; and, "You can see that things are coming out, after all, as I had envisioned them already last spring; my things are to be subordinated to yours, not the other way around." On January 15, 1918 she gave another lecture before the Mathematical Society in Göttingen, entitled, *Über Invarianten beliebiger Differentialausdrücke* (On invariants of arbitrary differential forms); on January 25 of the same year, F. Klein, at a regular meeting of the Königliche Gesellschaft der Wissenschaften (Royal Society for the Sciences), presented a paper with the title "Frl. E. Noether, *Über Differentialformen beliebigen Grades*" (On differential forms of arbitrary degree). On July 23, 1918, Emmy Noether spoke again before the Mathematical Society on the subject, *"Invariante Variations-*

probleme'' (Invariant variational problems); at the end of September of the same year she submitted the final version of the paper introduced by Klein. It was printed in the Göttinger Nachrichten of 1918, pp. 235–257, and was considered her *Habilitation* thesis. On May 21, 1919, the faculty was granted approval of the *Habilitation* request; on May 28 the oral examination followed, and on June 4, 1919, on Wednesday before Whitsuntide, Emmy Noether delivered her test lecture before the mathematical contingent of the philosophical faculty in Göttingen, consisting at that time of Courant (1888–1972), Debye (1884–1966), Hilbert, Klein, Landau, Prandtl (1875–1953), Runge (1856–1927), and Voigt (1850–1919), among others. The following excerpt from the hand-written curriculum vitae attached to Noether's *Habilitation* act may show how she herself characterized the works she had published or prepared for publication so far,

My dissertation and one later paper . . . still deal with the formal theory of invariants, which at that time was the natural subject for me as a student of Gordan. My greatest work, Fields and systems of rational functions ("Körper und Systeme rationaler Funktionen") is concerned with general questions on bases; it comes to terms with the problem of rational representability and contributes towards the solutions to the remaining questions of finiteness. One application of these results is found in my paper, The finiteness theorem for invariants of finite groups (*Der Endlichkeitssatz der Invarianten endlicher Gruppen*) which offers an absolutely elementary proof of finiteness by actually finding a basis. This same train of thought is continued in the paper, Algebraic equations with pre-assigned group (*Algebraische Gleichungen mit vorgeschriebener Gruppe*) which is a contribution to the construction of such equations for any field range . . . My paper, *Ganze rationale Darstellung von Invarianten* (Integral rational representation of invariants) demonstrates the truth of a conjecture stated by D. Hilbert and at the same time furnishes a purely conceptual proof of the serial developments of the theory of invariants, based on the equivalence between linear sets of forms and modelled in part on lines of reasoning of E. Fischer . . . Two further papers, unpublished as yet, also belong to this group of purely algebraic works; one is titled, *Ein Endlichkeitsbeweis für die ganzzahligen binären Invarianten* (A finiteness proof for integral binary invariants) . . . the other, co-authored by W. Schmeidler, is an investigation concerning noncommutative one-sided modules . . . My research concerning problems of algebra and module theory mod g should also be mentioned here as well as the problem of the alternative in nonlinear systems of equations . . . Another fairly large paper, *Die allgemeinsten Bereiche aus ganzen*

transzendenten Zahlen (The most general domains of transcendental integers) applies, in
addition to algebraic and arithmetical principles, those of abstract set theory . . . The
same direction is followed in the paper
Funktionalgleichungen und isomorphe Abbildung
(Functional equations and isomorphic mapping) which determines the most general
isomorphic mapping of any abstractly defined
field. The last two works to be mentioned here
concern differential invariants and variational
problems and in part are an outgrowth of my
assistance to Klein and Hilbert in their work on
Einstein's general theory of relativity . . .
The second of these papers, *Invariante Variationsprobleme* (Invariant variational problems), which I designated as my *Habilitation*
thesis, deals with arbitrary finite or infinite
continuous groups, in the sense of Lie, and dis-
closes what consequences it has for a variational problem to be invariant with respect to
such a group. The general results contain, as
special cases, the theorems on first integrals as
they are known in mechanics; furthermore,
the conservation theorems and the inter-
dependences among the field equations in
the theory of relativity—while, on the other
hand, the converse of these theorems is also
given . . .

The first course of lectures announced exclusively in the name of Dr. Emmy Noether
was given in 1919 during the intermediary
fall semester which had been specially or-

ganized for war veterans for the period from September 22 to December 20, representing a considerable addition to the workload of both professors and *Dozenten*. Noether's course was entitled Analytical Geometry, and was taught on Wednesdays and Saturdays from 11 A.M. to 1 P.M. Then, during the shortened winter semester 1919/20, following a Christmas vacation of only two weeks, Dr. Noether had the opportunity to teach a course from her own area of research. She repeated her four-hour lectures on algebraic and differential invariants in the following winter, 1921/22; in between, she "read" (as the expression in Germany goes) on higher algebra, finiteness theorems, theory of fields, elementary theory of numbers, and algebraic number fields; all of them four-hour lectures.

Opinions of Emmy Noether's lectures differ widely. Many of her students of that time became university professors themselves, some of them eminent ones. The most famous among them, considered by experts the greatest mathematician living today, remembers that he felt Noether's lectures to be poorly prepared, that he had difficulty following them, and that one time, in a lecture which ended at 1 P.M., he scribbled in the margin of his notebook, "It's 12:50, thank God!" Another professor who, as one of Noether's foremost pupils, established himself quickly and who, by his own account, is deeply indebted to her, feels that the one and only lecture he heard by her was by no means a "major experience" for him—as he had heard others say every single lecture of hers was. No doubt she transmitted the main inspiration to her students through personal conversation, which with her was unusually spirited. One opinion has it that her lectures were only enjoyable and profitable if one was already thoroughly acquainted with the subject and had accustomed oneself—with considerable effort, no doubt—to Noether's rather unique manner. Possibly it made a difference, too, whether she had to speak on traditional themes—which definitely went against the grain—or whether she was free to present her own, usually not yet fully developed, theories. The main reason, however, why Noether's lectures were judged in so many different ways is probably simply that her entirely abstract approach to algebra was not to everyone's taste, and that, while some students wished to be presented with clean, definite results arrived at by safe and sound argumentation, others enjoyed watching them take form, and participating in deriving and perfecting them. Emmy Noether provided plenty of opportunity for this, as is confirmed, for example, by B. L. van der Waerden, a favorite student of Noether, in his obituary (see p. 100).—At the same time, however, it must be kept in mind that van der Waerden was already a full-fledged mathematician, though young and eager to learn, when he came to Göttingen, and that E. Noether had already acquired several years practice in lecturing by that time, so that some of her initial difficulties might have been overcome. Furthermore, the lectures van der Waerden is referring to are obviously her special ones on hypercomplex quantities and group characters or on noncommutative algebra, while some of the other judgments may refer to basic courses she taught in beginning and intermediate semesters. In a conversation about Noether's lecturing habits, van der Waerden described the following typical scene: Emmy was supposed to demonstrate the theorem of Maschke (1853–1908). While she was preparing for the class she thought of a proof different from the usual one—one that would be constructed, following her preference for an abstract approach, entirely from concepts and axioms, involving no calculations at all and only little writing. While trying this out ahead of time she did not quite carry it through, but hoped that the proof as she envisioned it, based on her preparatory work, would come about while being developed in class. When she realized during her lecture that this was not going to happen, she was overcome by rage. Throwing her piece of chalk on the floor and stamping on it, she cried out, "There, I'm forced to do it the way I don't want to!" and proceeded to demonstrate Maschke's thesis faultlessly—in the "traditional manner."—A striking and surely appropriate evaluation of Noether's didactic abilities is contained in the petition addressed to the Ministry by the department of mathematics and natural sciences in 1922, requesting that Emmy Noether, now *Privatdozentin*, be given the official title of a *"ausserordentlicher Professor*." It reads: "Her renown as a scientist is indisputable . . . While less well suited as instructor of large classes in elementary disciplines, she is capable of exercising great scientific influence upon gifted students, many of whom she has furthered considerably, and some of whom have already achieved *Ordinariate*." From E. Noether herself we have a remark concerning her lectureship, in a letter to H. Hasse, "This winter I'm giving a course on the hypercomplex, which is as much fun for me as it is for my students."

Some amusing memories of Emmy are still in circulation today; for example, how she used to keep her handkerchief tucked into her bosom and, whenever needed, pull it out with a certain typical, unconcerned gesture, then tuck it back in. Her blouse easily became untidied by the animation with which she spoke, and gave daily cause for amusement.

The same was true for her hair, as long as she wore it pinned up. Even if it was neatly done when she entered the classroom, soon enough little wisps would begin to stick out here and there. Once, during the short break in the middle of a two hour class, two female students tried to draw Frl. Professor's attention to these defects in her appearance, but she was so absorbed in urgent discussion with students that they never got a chance, and so had to leave her to continue her lecture in a state of disarray. At times, "outsiders," that is, students who were not part of the Noether crowd, would come and try to follow one of her lectures. They would sit in the last rows, while the "regulars" sat in the front. Very often one of the latter would turn around in the first half-hour and announce, with satisfaction, "The enemy has been defeated; he has cleared out."

Emmy Noether often behaved in a manner less than friendly toward people who did not relate to her way of thinking, or even towards those whom she assumed did not. This has been reported by various parties. Nowadays no one bears a grudge against her for this. However, at the time people were often offended by her harsh and sometimes downright derisive manner. But when it came to helping someone, Emmy Noether was there with motherly unselfishness, always willing to share her wealth of ideas with anyone capable of understanding them, and often extending herself quite far. As a nonofficial member of the board of editors for the *Mathematische Annalen* she was not only conscientious and precise but also demonstrated the ability to give up her point of view whenever something less than essential was at stake. It is still said today that E. Noether's helpfulness was clearly reserved for those students who adhered to her teachings devotedly. While it may be that in some cases her behavior justified this rumor, a number of instances are also known which contradict it. One example is Karl Dörges' relationship with Emmy Noether. Although he was neither a pupil nor a collaborator, Noether, as editorial assistant of the *Mathematische Annalen*, provided much guidance for him in his first papers and thus influenced his method of working. The interest she took in his work intensified his own delight in the complex of thought surrounding Hilbert's irreducibility theorem. When he refused E. Noether's suggestion that he spend a semester in Göttingen, she did not change her behavior towards him in the least. She edited his last papers for the *Annalen* just as carefully as she had done the first ones, and her letters to him show that not only did she think highly of his abilities but she let him know it, too. Another collaborative relationship, that between Emmy Noether and the young number theorist Arnold Scholz (1904–1942), and the influence they had on each other, is described by Olga Taussky Todd in her obituary of Scholz, printed in *Mathematischen Nachrichten* (#7, 1952, p. 380). She writes, "He made less use of abstract algebra than others did. I know that Emmy Noether tried to win him over to her camp. He worked with her up to her death, and I believe that she would have succeeded if she had lived longer. On the other hand, he succeeded in making her see the beauty and significance of numerical examples which might be considered quite an achievement in view of her absolute devotion to abstract thinking."

Van der Waerden wrote, "She was both a loyal friend and a severe critic. It is these qualities which made her so valuable an editor too, for the *Mathematische Annalen*." (Obituary, p. 111). Hermann Weyl is of the opinion that Emmy Noether was hurt because her work for the *Mathematische Annalen* was never explicitly recognized, as was probably the case during her life time. On the other hand, the above-mentioned obituary by Professor van der Waerden, which praises Emmy Noether highly as a creative mathematician and outstanding person, did appear in *Mathematische Annalen*—the year was 1935, the country, Germany. The young generation of our day may not be aware of the meaning this carried. One must keep in mind that obituaries of other Jewish mathematicians who died during the Hitler regime did not appear in German publications until after, and often long after, 1945.

Vladimir Kořínek, professor in Prague, says in his obituary of Emmy Noether (1935), "Soon after the war she became involved with the first of the two problem complexes of modern algebra in which her research was to become truly significant. These two complexes—the general theory of ideals and the theory of noncommutative systems—were expanded by her into vast systems of thought." Actually, Noether's interest in the theory of modules and the theory of ideals goes back further, as is evident from her correspondence with E. Fischer and from the fact that in June 1917 she lectured before the Mathematical Society on Lasker's decomposition theorems of module theory. Her first publication on this subject, a treatise written in collaboration with W. Schmeidler (1890–1969), follows in 1920 in the *Mathematische Zeitschrift*. Interestingly enough, as Bourbaki later pointed out, it is in this work, which is on rings of differential operators, rather than in studies on algebras, that the terms "right and left ideal" (N. Bourbaki, Eléments d'histoire des mathématiques, Paris 1960, p. 126) first appear. When Schmeidler, sometime later, was praised by someone for the clarity of his lectures and the beauty of thought expressed in them, he objected, indicating that he owed much of what might appear to be his own to somebody else. The informed person knew that he meant Emmy Noether.

In October 1920, while in Erlangen, Noether submitted to the *Mathematische Annalen* another paper of fundamental importance for the further development of algebra, *Idealtheorie in Ringbereichen* (The Theory of Ideals in *Ringbereichen*). The crucial discovery demonstrated in this paper was, to quote W. Krull, "that the major decomposition theorems by Lasker and Macaulay can be derived in a most translucent manner, and generalized to a high degree, solely by means of the ascending chain condition (*Teilerkettensatz*) originated by Dedekind."

Just as she had returned to Erlangen because of her mother's death in 1915, Emmy Noether went there several more times in the following years to bury other loved ones—in 1918, her brother Alfred; in 1921, her father; in 1928, her youngest brother. She did this with remarkable composure, dealing with them quietly, surely not without sorrow and grief, yet keeping it all to herself. With the same readiness with which she responded to anything offering the least bit of joy, she faced disagreeable and painful occurrences as a natural part of life. Her true generosity of heart became particularly evident when, in

1933, her friends and acquaintances suffered the same tragic fate as she did. It was their predicament she was concerned about, not her own. She tried her best to encourage them with her own optimism, and showed how deeply grateful she was for every bit of help she received from non-Jewish friends.

After the deaths in her family, the only close relatives left were her brother Fritz, *Professor Ordinarius* in Breslau, and his family. She was always on close terms with him; she often spent parts of her vacation with his family and was especially fond of the younger of the two sons, Gottfried. She was never sentimental in expressing her affections but almost rough, in a jolly way. Yet she always spoke of this nephew with obvious emotion, and perhaps some pride because he showed mathematical talent at a very young age. As a preschooler he had already declared that, if a professor was someone having to do with numbers, that was what he wanted to become. And he did. However, he was only twenty years old when his aunt died, so that she only knew him up to the beginning of his studies—and that under the sad conditions of emigration, with her living in the U.S. and he in Siberia (where his father had obtained a position as professor at the Research Institute for Mathematics and Mechanics in Tomsk).

Emmy's simple and modest way of life was a phenomenon well known in Göttingen and

Erlangen. What was probably simply a natural inclination of hers became a necessary asset because in Germany she at first received no salary from the state at all, and only a very small one from 1923 on. Even after inflation she still had a small inheritance, but she only used it for the support of her youngest brother. In 1933 when she and others were dismissed from their positions by the Prussian government without a pension or any other compensation, she immediately thought of those who had less than she had, if anything at all, to get them through the immediate future. On May 10, 1933 she writes to Helmut Hasse, "Many thanks for your dear, compassionate letter! I must say, though, that this thing is much less terrible for me than it is for many others. At least I have a small inheritance (I never was entitled to a pension, anyway) which allows me to sit back for a while and see." In the United States she received the salary of a visiting professor, which couldn't have been very much. But compared to the remuneration received by a *nichtbeamteter ausserordentlicher Professor mit Lehrauftrag** in Prussia, and considering her modest needs, it was a substantial amount. When one of her acquaintances from Göttingen met her in Princeton in 1935

---

* *nichtbeamteter ausserordentlicher Professor mit Lehrauftrag:* professor without tenure.

and said that now she could finally live it up a little, she exclaimed, "Oh no! What do you think! I only use half of it, the rest I'm saving for my nephew!" A simple pleasure—not to be granted her much longer.

Emmy's attitude towards material goods is reflected in a whole series of authenticated details and anecdotes. Once, in Göttingen, she was walking with some of her students in the rain. Although she did have an umbrella, it was of little use, and her companions were embarrassed about the state it was in. Finally, one of them suggested that Frau Professor have it repaired sometime. To this Emmy Noether replied, "Quite right, but it can't be done: when it doesn't rain I don't think of the umbrella, and when it rains I need it." Sometimes she wore shoes so sturdy that one could not avoid the impression that they were men's. But she was open to friendly reproach. Once, when she had already achieved the status of an *ausserordentlicher Professor*, a good friend suggested that it was time to replace her wardrobe, and she took his advice. Her eating habits, too, caused her friends amusement. The story goes that every day Emmy Noether was to be found not only sitting in the same place at the same time in the same humble restaurant, but also eating the same plain meal. She did cook, though, in the small kitchen of her attic apartment, but only on Sundays and always in the company

of her *"Trabanten"* (squires)—at least during
the time when those *"Trabanten"* were
Heinrich Grell (1903–1974) and Rudolf
Hölzer (who died in 1926 at the age of
twenty-three). On Sunday afternoons they
took walks together, constantly talking
mathematics. Giving and taking through scientific discourse with others was characteristic of Emmy Noether's way of teaching. In
the evening the party would return to the
Düstere Eichenweg ("Somber Oaks Way")
—later to the Friedländer Weg—in order
to cook pudding à la Noether—without
interrupting their algebraic conversation. The
pudding always tasted the same—delicious.
Afterwards, the kitchen was left as it was.
Sometime later a cleaning woman would
come to rinse the dried pudding remains
from the dishes. Taking walks in the pretty
country around their town was one of the
customs of the Göttingen mathematicians.
With Emmy Noether these walks tended to
be especially long—and they didn't end with
refreshments at an inn, either! When the
group became tired, they simply sat down in
a meadow or at the edge of a wood and continued the discussion. Heinrich Kapferer
(Freiburg i. Br.) remembered such a walk
even in his old age and described it very
humorously in a letter. Kapferer, by the way
(whom Emmy addressed as *Herr Vetter*
(cousin) on account of his relationship to her

brother Fritz's wife), was one of those all-too-rare people who judged and treated Noether fairly without being attracted in the least to her way of thinking. On the occasion of his fiftieth birthday, H. Kapferer wrote an interesting essay called *Kurven in meinem Leben* (Curves in My Life) in which, unconcerned about the attitudes of his contemporaries (it was the year 1938!) he dared frankly to acknowledge Emmy Noether's contributions to abstract algebra and freely to admit how he himself had profited from his conversations with her.

The course of E. Noether's official career after her *Habilitation* in 1919 is as follows. On April 6, 1922, the Prussian Minister of Science, Art and Public Education presented Fräulein Dr. Emmy Noether with a document attributing to her the official title of *ausserordentlicher Professor*. The text of this document literally states that this act was being carried out ". . . with the understanding that this title does not signify any change in your present legal position. In particular, your relations to your faculty as they ensued from your position as a *Privatdozentin* will remain untouched; neither does this title entail the assignment of any officially authorized function." In other words, it was a "title without means" (*Titel ohne Mittel*); it was the least the Ministry could do for Emmy Noether. As a result of some pressure from the Mathematics Department, and the "accidental" failure to forward a certain letter, E. Noether received a contract, dated April 22, 1923, for teaching algebra, including lectures and exercises, which at last provided her with a small, steady income. It also meant that she was now officially permitted to see her students through to their final examinations; as a consequence, a series of dissertations was inspired and fostered by her. The first doctoral dissertation by a Noether student in Göttingen was that of Grete Hermann who took her examinations in February 1925 with E. Noether and E. Landau. Even today Frau Dr. Henry-Hermann remembers her "dissertation-mother" with deep reverence, and delights in cheerful memories of her. She has not forgotten E. Noether's many gestures of motherly kindness and care towards her students as well as towards those colleagues who were subject to unjust treatment.

Almost simultaneously with Grete Hermann, Rudolf Hölzer and Heinrich Grell (who, after many digressions, became professor at Humboldt University in Berlin, and died in 1974) also wrote their doctoral dissertations under the guidance of Emmy Noether. Rudolf Hölzer died of tuberculosis at the age of 23, just before receiving his degree, yet after having completed his dissertation. Heinrich Grell (who obtained his doctor's degree in 1926) was held in high esteem by his teacher and enjoyed the privilege of her support even after graduation. According to him, E. Noether had directed his "inclinations to the right channels" by familiarizing him with Dedekind. His name is the only one in Poggendorff's literary biographical handbook listed with the notation, "Student of Emmy Noether." Heinrich Grell was always aware that he owed much to Emmy Noether and often expressed this in public, as on the occasion of the memorial held for Hermann Weyl in 1965, and in 1952 during the commemoration of Emmy Noether's seventieth birthday at his Institute in Berlin. Thanks to H. Grell, Emmy Noether's paper *Idealdifferentiation und Differente* (Ideal differentiation and the different) was post-humously published in the *Journal für die reine und angewandte Mathematik* (188, 1950, pp. 1–21). Emmy Noether had given a lecture about this work at the congress in Prague in 1929. Her original draft for it, only in part prepared for printing and temporarily intended for the *Herbrand-Gedächtnis-Band* (Herbrand Memorial Edition), is one of the few unpublished manuscripts she left behind. In 1929 Werner Weber obtained a doctor's degree with his thesis, *Idealtheoretische Deutung der Darstellbarkeit beliebiger natürlicher Zahlen durch quadratische Formen* (The representability of arbitrary natural numbers by quadratic forms, interpreted from the theory of ideals). The reviewers were E. Landau and E. Noether. Weber thanked Noether especially for her generous assistance. He was followed two weeks later by Jakob Levitzki (from Tel Aviv) whose thesis had also been initiated and fostered by Noether, and who also was examined by Noether and Landau. The miserable financial situation of this gifted young man, who was born in Russia and later had emigrated to Palestine with his parents, particularly concerned Emmy Noether. She did all she could to find a position for him as *Assistent*—an extremely difficult undertaking since he was both a foreigner and a Jew, although described by her as "unusually capable and likeable . . . with nothing unpleasantly Jewish about him." At last Levitzki received a Sterling Fellowship at Yale University in New Haven, Connecticut, and eventually became very successful both in America and Palestine. He mostly worked in the theory of rings, partly in collaboration with S. Amitsur. He died at the age of about fifty. Another "Noether boy" was Max Deuring, who graduated in 1930; according to some comments in Noether's letters, even as an undergraduate she considered him the most promising of her students to become a member of the next generation of Göttingen mathematicians. Deuring's student years coincided with a period which was particularly exciting for the study of abstract algebra, a time when Emmy Noether "was without doubt the strongest center of mathematical activity there, considering both the fertility of her research program and her influence upon a large circle of pupils." (Cf. H. Weyl, Memorial Address, pp. 127–128). After her emigration, Emmy Noether expressed the wish that her teaching assignment be transferred to Deuring, although he was still very young then and not yet *habilitiert*. The great expectations she had of Max Deuring as an algebraist were brilliantly fulfilled. His extensive report, *Algebren* (Algebras), published in 1935 in the collection *Ergebnisse der Mathematik und ihrer Grenzgebiete* (Results of mathematics and its adjoining fields) met with Noether's liveliest interest. Sadly, she did not live long enough to witness the further development of her pupil. After serving as *Ordinarius* in Marburg and Hamburg, Max Deuring held an *ordentlicher Lehrstuhl* at the University in Göttingen until he became emeritus.

Another of Noether's doctoral candidates who gave cause for high hopes was Hans Fitting, who received his degree in 1931. His dissertation on automorphism rings and another paper entitled *Über die direkten Produktzerlegungen einer Gruppe in direkt unzerlegbare Faktoren* (On the direct product decompositions of a group into directly indecomposable factors) were greatly appreciated by Noether. She obtained a grant for him from the *Notgemeinschaft der Deutschen Wissenschaften* (Emergency Society for German Sciences) which allowed him to continue his work in Göttingen and Leipzig until he was *habilitiert* in Königsberg. He died in 1938, barely 32 years of age, from a rapidly advancing bone disease. His name lives on in the literature of algebraic structure theory, embodied in the terms Fitting's lemma and Fitting's radical. Emmy Noether commented about another student of hers, Ernst Witt, now *Ordinarius*, "He suddenly has begun to work, rather than just to simplify." The time of Witt's doctoral candidacy—July 1933—coincided with the beginning of the regime. For this reason Herglotz (1881–1953) was assigned as reviewer to his thesis, although the subject, Riemann-Roch theorem and zeta functions in hypercomplex systems, belonged to the area of research of Noether, Hasse, and F. K. Schmidt.

Nothing is known so far about what became of the Chinese student, Chiungtze Tsen, whose dissertation *"Algebren über Funktionenkörpern* (Algebras over function fields) was also inspired and tirelessly supported by E. Noether. However, he took his examinations after the emigration of his benefactress. In 1936 a paper by him *"Zur*

Stufentheorie der quasi-algebraisch-Abgeschlossenheit kommutativer Körper'' (On the step theory of quasi-algebraic closedness of commutative fields) (as reported by N. Jacobson in *Theory of Rings* (New York City 1943)) appeared in the Journal of the Chinese Mathematical Society (v. 1, pp. 81–92), from which one might conclude that Tsen may have returned to his country.

The last doctoral candidate from the Göttingen circle to be mentioned here, who was given inspiration and counsel by E. Noether (and her close collaborator, Helmut Hasse), is Otto Schilling (1911–1973). He emigrated in 1935—by choice—to the United States, where he became productive in the field of abstract algebra. Probably his best–known work is his book on valuation theory. His interest in this subject evolved from his studies with Hasse on the pioneering works of Hensel (1861–1941), Krull, and Ostrowski. Just before the end of her activity in Göttingen, Emmy Noether mentioned another doctoral candidate. On June 27, 1933, she writes: "I must hurriedly look through a dissertation (Schwarz) which officially is assigned to Weyl." Later there was to be one more graduate, a woman, at E. Noether's new place of work, the women's college—or "Weiber-College", by her own translation—of Bryn Mawr.

The term "the Noether school" does not

refer as much to the large group of Noether's doctoral students as it does to the group of mathematicians who basically shared Noether's mathematical approach and in this spirit contributed to the development of abstract algebra, often working Independently of the master, often in intense exchange, and occasionally in close collaboration with her. First on this list is Wolfgang Krull, who introduced Noether's mode of thinking at the University of Freiburg in Breisgau. Here F. K. Schmidt and Reinhold Baer, both algebraists of distinction, came under its influence. Another "Noether boy" was the Austrian Gottfried Köthe who after his graduation came to Göttingen to continue his studies. Köthe actively participated in the new development of the theory of hypercomplex quantities, initiated by Artin and Noether, and continued in the methods of Noether's abstract theory of ideals and those of Krull's general theory of groups. Köthe was one of those mathematicians who eventually developed his own ideas but always remained true to the spirit of the Noether school.

B. L. van der Waerden has already been mentioned several times. His two-volume textbook on algebra is more widely used than any other work in this subject. Even its 7th edition includes the notation: "Based in part on lectures by E. Artin and E. Noether." The introduction specifies which lectures are re-

ferred to. "Van der Waerden came to her
from Holland as a more or less finished
mathematician and with ideas of his own;
but he learned from Emmy Noether the apparatus of notions and the kind of thinking
that permitted him to formulate his ideas and
to solve his problems." (Cf. H. Weyl, Memorial Address, pp. 112-152). Van der Waerden's obituary of Emmy Noether (pp. 100–111
in this book) makes it clear that he was enthusiastic not only about her subject matter
but probably even more so about her treatment of it. The clarity of her conceptualiza-
tion and the nearly total abstraction of her
thinking excited and influenced him deeply.
It is remarkable that already at the time of
her death, without the benefit of an objective
distance from her work, he was able to
characterize her mathematical intellect with
such precision. Thirty years later, in a speech
on the history of algebra since Galois, delivered to the Deutsche Mathematiker-Vereinigung (German Mathematical Association)
on its 75th anniversary, van der Waerden
called the years from 1920 to 1934 "one of
the great periods of algebra," with Emmy
Noether, Emil Artin, and Alexander Ostrowski opening up new frontiers. In this
speech van der Waerden once again sum-
marized Emmy Noether's work in algebra
and showed its place in the overall development of abstract algebra.

Emmy Noether en route from Swinemünde to Königsberg (aboard the steamship "Danziq") to attend the annual meeting of the DMV, September, 1930. The photo was taken by H. Hasse

Postcard to E. Fischer (postmarked April 10, 1915, Erlangen)

Köthe, Emmy Noether, and Artin, in front of the Mathematical Institute, Göttingen.

van der Waerden, Emmy Noether, 1929

Starting with Dedekind's theory of ideals, and using theorems by Hilbert, Lasker, and Macaulay, E. Noether succeeded in forming the foundations of the general theory of ideals, to which W. Krull was to make significant contributions later on. Furthermore, E. Noether established necessary and sufficient conditions for every ideal to be a product of powers of prime ideals (five-axiom-ring, or Dedekind ring). By eliminating individual axioms, van der Waerden,

Prüfer (1896–1934), and Artin obtained generalizations. The most far-reaching generalization of Dedekind's theory of ideals—a purely multiplicative ideal theory for integrally closed rings—was produced by Paul Lorenzen. Another generalization—by Heinrich Brandt (1886–1954)—concerned the theory of ideals of noncommutative algebras, which in turn provided Artin with the foundation for his general substantiation of the arithmetic of algebras. Van der Waerden also mentions his own foundation of algebraic geometry, which is based not only on Steinitz's field theory and Mertens' resultants for homogeneous forms, but also on the theory of ideals as formulated by Lasker and Noether.

It must be added here that Emmy Noether was always very interested in the foundation of algebraic geometry and that she herself made valuable contributions to it. Incidentally, it is in this area that one of the typical incidents occurred which show E. Noether's generous attitude concerning the authorship of publications. Kurt Hentzelt had written a dissertation in Erlangen; it was complete but not ready for printing when the war broke out in 1914. The young man received his doctor's degree just before he was sent to the Western Front. In October 1914 he was already reported missing in action. In 1921, in the Annual Report of the DMV, E. Noether briefly mentioned Hentzelt's paper, then published a revised version of it in the *Mathematische Annalen* with the title, *Zur Theorie der Polynomideale und Resultanten* (On the theory of polynomial ideals and resultants). In her lectures during the winter of 1923/24 and the following summer, she elaborated further on Hentzelt's ideas, and achieved beautiful results. When B. L. van der Waerden came to Göttingen in the fall of 1924, he read Noether's revised version of Hentzelt's work on elimination theory in the *Annalen* and received from it a very important impetus toward constructing the zero field of a prime ideal by forming residue classes and quotients, as well as towards the possibility of specialization of the general zeros. It was only after van der Waerden had drawn these conclusions from Hentzelt's ideas that he was shown by H. Grell how it had been worked out by Emmy Noether in her lectures. She had developed exactly the same chain of thought as van der Waerden. In agreement, though independent of each other, both had developed the same clear, fundamental concepts from a given theory, and arrived at the same conclusions. Emmy Noether did not claim any right to priority, but withdrew and left publication of the findings to her younger colleague. His paper appeared in volume 96 of the *Mathematische Annalen* with the title, *"Zur Nullstellentheorie der Polynomideale"* (Theory of zeroes of polynomial ideals). In 1948, in his contribution to "Studies and Essays Presented to R. Courant on his 60th Birthday" (January 8, 1948, New York 1948), entitled, "The Foundation of Algebraic Geometry: A Very Incomplete Historical Survey," van der Waerden himself verifies what Emmy Noether's and his own role were in the foundation of algebraic geometry.

After a brief survey of the theory of valuations, in his memorial address of 1965 van der Waerden discusses the tendency of viewing algebraic structures as groups with operators and strongly emphasizes that this approach could be clearly recognized in E. Noether's work from the start.

This speech, which in spite of its brevity contains far more than has been implied here, seems to confirm a thought which E. Noether expressed about herself in 1931. In a letter to Hasse she wrote, "My methods are really methods of working and thinking; this is why they have crept in everywhere anonymously." Shortly after her death, H. Hopf (1894–1971) and P. Alexandrov wrote in the preface to their Topology (Berlin 1935), "Emmy Noether's general mathematical insights were not confined to her specialty—algebra—but affected anyone who came in touch with her work." Thirty years later at the colloquium on topology in Brussels, and again a year later at the anniversary meeting of the DMV in 1965—where van der Waerden also spoke, as mentioned above—Heinz Hopf expressed in truly moving words his grateful appreciation of Emmy Noether's direct and indirect influence on the algebraization of topology. He mentioned his friendship with Alexandrov and called that time happy and very cheerful. Emmy Noether would probably have joined him in that description. She, too, was a friend of Alexandrov's, and her natural cheeriness contributed much to their friendship. Alexandrov, *ordentlicher Professor* at the University of Moscow since 1924 and speaking German fluently, came to Germany repeatedly as a visiting professor, mostly to Göttingen, and would have liked to obtain a professorship in Germany. In vain Emmy Noether tried to help him with this rather hopeless plan. She was more successful in her attempt to obtain a Rockefeller fellowship for Alexandrov and Hopf through Hermann Weyl, which enabled both topologists to spend the academic year of 1927/28 with the leading topologists Veblen and Lefschetz (1884–1972) in Princeton.

Emmy Noether spent the winter of 1928/ 29 and the beginning of the following summer semester as a visiting professor in Moscow and felt very much at ease there in the circle of Alexandrov and his friends. Upon her return she was all admiration and enthusiasm for her stay in Moscow, which prompted some spiteful people to the remark, "Emmy, of course, with her nearsightedness hasn't noticed a thing!" Two publications— both in German—appeared in the Reports of the Moscow Mathematical Society as a result of E. Noether's stay there, one by Noether herself on *Maximalbereiche aus ganzzahligen Funktionen* (Maximal domains of integral functions), the other written by I. Arnold (1900–1948), under the influence of Noether and Khintchin (1895–1959), on *Ideale in kommutativen Halbgruppen* (Ideals in commutative semigroups). E. Noether also lectured in Moscow (on abstract algebra) as mentioned in a paper by L. S. Pontrjagin which, inspired by Alexandrov and Noether, was published in the *Mathematische Annalen*. (Pontrjagin was still very young when Noether was in Moscow; he became professor at the University of Moscow in 1935.)

One of the Russian scholars frequenting Noether's circle in Göttingen and participating in the stimulating exchange of ideas was Otto Julewitsch Schmidt (1891–1956), arctic explorer, organizer of the Northern sea route, geophysicist, and mathematician. His personality was described by Heinrich Grell as "radiating a sense of primal vigor and broadness." Following Krull, and using Noether's methods, Schmidt contributed to the theory of infinite groups with finite chain, and essentially to the advancement of algebra in the USSR. Ten years after his death, the Soviet Union issued a postage stamp honoring his seventy-fifth birthday.

Among E. Noether's acquaintances in Russia to whom she sent copies of her publications were W. W. Stepanow (1889–1950) who was in Göttingen in 1927, and N. G. Tschebotaröw (1894–1947). In his book *Grundzüge der Galoisschen Theorie* (Major aspects of Galois theory) translated from the Russian and completed by H. Schwerdtfeger in 1950, Tschebotaröw devotes considerable space to Noether's contributions to Galois theory and emphasizes the marked advancement of algebra ever since it became abstract and gained recognition through the works of E. Noether and her school.

However, not only Russians came from abroad to the "world center of mathematics," as Göttingen was called. There was hardly a country that was not represented by students, young Ph.D.s, and professors, in Germany, and particularly in Göttingen, to study and pursue research for long and short periods. There were, of course, a number of outstanding figures in Göttingen besides E. Noether who attracted these guests, Landau, Carathéodory (1873–1950), Courant, Herglotz, at times also H. Weyl, and always especially Hilbert. But few of these had an impact as far-reaching and lasting as Emmy

Noether. Among the guests from Japan, Kenjiro Shoda should be mentioned first. An accomplished mathematician, he came from Tokyo where he had graduated in 1925, and became such a close follower of Noether's teachings that after his return he became the chief representative of abstract algebra in Japan. He also wrote two remarkable books on that subject. Shoda and his teacher Takagi are considered among the most eminent Japanese mathematicians. Suetuna (1898–1970), also from Tokyo, was in Göttingen in 1928 and 1929 and frequented Noether's circle there. Many other Japanese scholars contributed to the further development of abstract algebra in the spirit of the Noether school; every bibliography of modern algebra contains a list of Japanese authors.

In France, the more recent aspects of mathematics, such as Hilbert's investigations into the foundations of mathematics, the theory of ideals, topology, and algebraic geometry, had been neglected. In a letter to Hasse in 1928 Emmy Noether mentions that Châtelet (1883–1960) was the only French scholar who was seriously concerned with the problems which she and her followers were working with. This situation changed when, supported by scholarships, a number of young, open-minded, and highly gifted Frenchmen were able to study abroad, especially in Germany, and, receiving fresh inspiration there, began to open up new directions of mathematical research in France. In the early thirties an intense exchange began to take place between Claude Chevalley on the one hand and Hasse and Noether on the other. Chevalley's paper on norm residues (*Comptes Rendus de l'Académie*, Paris, 1930), for example, was inspired by E. Noether's lectures of the winter semester 1929/30. André Weil, brother of the unforgettable Simone Weil (1909–1943) and presently probably the most famous pupil of E. Cartan, went to Germany to continue his studies, which deepened his involvement with abstract thought. One student with a Rockefeller grant, outstanding even among his brilliant peers, was Jacques Herbrand (1908–1931) who had been a student of Vessiot (1865–1952) in Paris. In 1931, while working with Artin in Hamburg, with John von Neumann (1903–1957) in Berlin, and finally with E. Noether in Göttingen, he amazed the mathematical world with his contributions, especially in the field of metamathematics. What brought him to Emmy Noether was his interest in the theory of ideals, an area in which he also did valuable work. Herbrand lectured before the Mathematical Societies of Berlin, Halle, and Göttingen. Emmy Noether was full of praise for his abilities, and his personality impressed all who knew him. In July 1931, he left Göttingen to go hiking in the

French Alps where he lost his life in an accident at twenty-three. Along with many others, Emmy Noether was profoundly shaken by the fate of this extraordinarily promising young mathematician. Weeks later she wrote, "I can't get Herbrand's death out of my mind." In volume 106 of the *Mathematische Annalen* (1932), E. Noether published a few results of the theory of algebraic functions which Herbrand had written to her. Following the suggestion of Claude Chevalley and André Weil, Herbrand's friends published a series of articles dedicated to him in the *Actualités Scientifiques et Industrielles*; among them is Emmy Noether's last work published before her death, *"Zerfallende verschränkte Produkte und ihre Maximalordnungen"* (Splitting crossed products and their maximal orders) (Paris 1934).

In 1930−32 the *Collected Mathematical Works* of Richard Dedekind were published. They were edited by Robert Fricke (1861−1930), Öystein Ore (1899−1958), and Emmy Noether. A biography of Dedekind by Fricke, who had known him personally, was supposed to be included, but Fricke died before it was written. Only a very minor part of the extensive commentaries are by Fricke; the great bulk is by Noether and Ore. (Ore, incidentally, is the author of a little book, *Algèbre abstraite* (Paris, 1936), which is very easy to understand even for beginners.) On his death, Dedekind left no less than fifty portfolios to be examined by the editors of his works. The commentaries by Noether not only show her profound familiarity with Dedekind's ideas but in part represent her own contributions towards their further development. A special "favorite" of Noether's was the so-called Eleventh Appendix to Dirichlet's lectures on number theory which she liked to recommend to her students and frequently referred to with the remark, "that's already noted in Dedekind." (*"Es steht schon bei Dedekind."*) Incidentally, in 1964 the Vieweg publishing company reprinted part of the third volume of Dedekind's Mathematical Works including E. Noether's commentaries with the title, *"Über die Theorie der ganzen algebraischen Zahlen"* (On the theory of algebraic integers). The introduction by van der Waerden gives a brief historical survey of the theory of ideals.

In collaboration with the young Frenchman Jean Cavaillès* (who joined the underground resistance in France and was killed by the Nazis in 1944), Emmy Noether edited the correspondence between G. Cantor and R. Dedekind, including the letters found in

---

* Cavaillès' portrait became widely known because of a postage stamp issued in 1958 as one in the *2e série des Héros de la Résistance,* although with no indication of his merits as a scientist.

Dedekind's estate. This work was completed in March 1933 but the small volume was not published until 1937, as issue #518 of the *Actualités Scientifiques et Industrielles,* edited by Hermann, Paris. In his preface (written in French), Cavaillès reminisces about the good old days in Göttingen and remembers Emmy Noether for her cheerful kindness and hospitality and the radiance of her unusual mind.

In the summer of 1931, at the same time as J. Herbrand and A. Weil, Solomon Lefschetz from Princeton (USA) was also in Göttingen. He, too, was a mathematician who thought like Noether. Another Princeton professor sympathetic to Noether's thinking was Oswald Veblen who was in Germany in 1932, and later of great help to the emigrant mathematicians. His specialty was geometry but in the area of differential invariants his interest touched upon Noether's, while as a topologist he was closer to Alexandrov and Hopf.

The number of American mathematicians visiting Göttingen was increasing from year to year. In 1929 a new Institute was built for the mathematics department on Bunsenstrasse (where they still work and teach today). The means for building and endowing came from the International Education Board founded by Rockefeller. A number of small rooms were provided for the *Privatdozenten* and *Assistenten,* nicknamed "*Kabuffs*" in the Göttingen academic slang. Emmy Noether's *"Kabuff"* was actually a little more spacious than the others. According to an observation by H. Hasse, Courant felt that this bit of favoritism was called for in the case of Noether's unique genius.

The persons in charge of the negotiations concerning the design and interior organization of the new building, and also of matters concerning the increasing exchange of professors between Germany and America, were G. D. Birkhoff (in America) and Richard Courant (in Germany). Courant had succeeded Hilbert as director of the Mathematical Institute in 1920 or 1921. This office not only was a great honor but also involved heavy responsibility and a considerable workload. Emmy Noether, it seems, had little appreciation of Courant's position. To her, mathematical work and the free-flowing exchange of ideas with friends was all that mattered; preoccupation with practical matters—inevitable for an enterprise of world-renown such as the Göttingen Institute had become—she derisively labelled "Gschaftelhuberei" (an untranslatable expression which, judging by its sound, she might have picked up in Austria). In her sometimes thoughtless manner of blurting out her thoughts she used this word with reference to Courant at some highly inappropriate moments, which caused an unpleasant situation for her. Fairly often people were bothered by her bluntness and perhaps by her generally noisy manner. But anyone who came to know her better was bound to realize warm-heartedness beneath the rugged surface. Erich Hecke (1887 1947), for example, wrote to Hermann Weyl soon after E. Noether's death, "I have learned to appreciate Emmy Noether deeply in the last years on the occasion of her several visits to Hamburg; she was a truly magnificent fellow. I must confess that at first I found it difficult to abstain from certain obvious facts . . ." It must be observed that Hecke had known E. Noether in Göttingen already when he was an *Assistent*, and again in 1919, but apparently he did not recognize her for what she was until later. This may have been true for many people. But whether or not she came to be liked as a person, her mathematical achievements were gradually recognized everywhere. Already by about 1925 it was quite clear that Emmy Noether had something to say and to give. How is it, then, that in her academic career she did not go beyond the level of a *nicht-beamteter ausserordentlicher Professor*? There probably were a number of reasons for this. It is impossible now, as it was then, to determine which one was decisive. Was it because she was Jewish? There were several Jewish *Ordinarii* in Göttingen. Was it because she was a member of the social-democratic party? She left the party in 1924 (after having been, according to her own account, a member of the Independent Social-Democratic Party of Germany from 1919–1922; later of the Social-Democratic Party of Germany). Could it be that this was held against her for so long? Or was it her firm stance as a pacifist that was frowned upon? Or did she, after all, lack the necessary scientific qualifications? Even if she was not especially talented as an instructor, she certainly ranked high above average as a researcher and scholar, as was confirmed by her colleagues in the petitions they submitted to the faculty on her behalf. Or was it her being a woman that made her undesirable as a faculty member? There is no clear implication or proof of the latter. It is a known fact that in Prague, after the First World War, a female *Assistent* in geography was refused *Habilitierung* because "the first *Dozentin* at the German University must not be named Moscheles." Possibly in Göttingen it was felt—unadmittedly—that the first female *Ordentlicher Professor* must not be named Noether. But there is another plausible explanation for Noether's remaining at the level of *Dozentin:* that she herself did not desire the position of an *Ordinarius* because she preferred her freedom. In that position she would have been obliged to teach basic courses and exercises for which she was not well suited. Much of her time would have been absorbed by preparations for classes, and her own research would have suffered. We can only guess at the reasons. What definitely was unfair, however, is that Emmy Noether was not elected into the *Gesellschaft der Wissenschaften* (the Göttingen Academy of Sciences). This opinion is held by leading mathematicians even today, including some who did not belong to Noether's circle.

The year 1932 did bring at last a token of recognition for Emmy Noether. Together with Artin she received the "Alfred Ackermann-Teubner memorial award for the advancement of the mathematical sciences"—an amount of RM 500. (about $120) for the whole of her scientific achievement.

In the same year, the Göttingen algebraists celebrated Emmy Noether's fiftieth birthday. In spite of her modesty, this sign of awareness from her colleagues did make her happy. What she enjoyed most was the paper Helmut Hasse dedicated to her in the *Mathematische Annalen*. It contains a noncommutative derivation of the law of reciprocity and confirms Noether's stated thought that the theory of noncommutative algebras is governed by simpler laws than is the theory of commutative algebras. A charming birthday gift was the m$\mu\nu$–riddle of syllables which Emmy, of course, solved instantly—and ate, as she writes to Hasse in her very cordial thank-you note. What exactly this riddle of syllables was about we will probably never know, since its author, following a recommendation by Hilbert, forgot it at once in order to make room for new knowledge in his learned brain!

Another meaningful event took place in September, 1932: the international congress of mathematicians in Zurich, Switzerland. It was something like a great family reunion with everyone of any standing in the mathematical world present, and in addition, many novices who had only just begun their service to the queen of the sciences. They came from all over the globe, to tell or hear about the newest results of research, to meet men and women personally with whom they had been acquainted only through the literature so far, and to renew and deepen old friendships. There were 247 official delegates and 420 participants, all in all, including others who attended, about 800 people. H. Weyl was there representing the DMV; Landau, Göttingen Academy; Courant, the Georg August University in Göttingen; Hasse, the University of Marburg; Haupt and Krull, the University of Erlangen—to mention only a few from the long list of prominent names. Emmy Noether was the only woman to give one of the twenty-one plenary lectures or *"grosse Vorträge"* (big lectures), as they were called. On September 7 she spoke on "Hypercomplex systems in their relations to com-

International Congress of Mathematicians, Zurich, 1932. (Emmy Noether appears not to be in this picture, although she attended the Congress. Many other well-known mathematicians are present.)

Deuring, Emmy Noether, Köthe, Hebrand, at the Sheaf Theory Congress, Marburg, February 26–28, 1931.

Olga Taussky (Todd), Göttingen, 1932

mutative algebra and to number theory (*Hyperkomplexe Systeme in ihren Beziehungen zur kommutativen Algebra und zur Zahlentheorie*). Immediately before going to the congress, she enjoyed a vacation in Wengen in the Bernese Alps and afterwards again allowed herself a few days of relaxation before the start of the next semester.

Soon after the congress trouble began in Göttingen. It not only affected people's personal lives but the department of mathematics and physics as such, and the future of science in general. Emmy Noether was among the first ones suspended by the Hitler regime. She was seen as especially "dangerous" because she had once—or was it several times?—offered her apartment as a meeting place for a leftist group of students. The official suspension from the representative of the Prussian Ministry of Science, Art and Public Education, dated April 2, 1933, and numbered U I Nr. 17277, reads as follows: "With reference to § 3 of the statutes for professional civil servants of April 7, 1933, I herewith withdraw your permission to teach at the University of Göttingen." The same verdict struck Max Born and Richard Courant. Others, such as Neugebauer, Landau, Bernays (1888–1979) were asked to cancel their lectures for the time being and withdraw from all other official activities. Since

Courant was declared unendurable Hermann Weyl became director of the Institute. Weyl was immediately in touch with Princeton in the hope of arranging a visiting lectureship there for Emmy Noether. While the decision was pending, Noether's circle of friends met privately in her apartment on Stegemühlenweg in order to discuss preparing lectures on Hasse's work on class field theory. Supposedly it did not bother Emmy Noether that one student—whom she liked—participated in this private session wearing the SA uniform. In June, Hasse and Noether exchanged letters about the hypercomplex interpretation of class field theory, as well as about testimonials which Hasse was collecting for E. Noether to be submitted, along with his own appeal, to the Minister in hopes of changing his mind. One four-page letter by Noether, dated July 1933, deals with division algebras, cyclicity, class field theory in hypercomplex set-up and various other algebraic and arithmetic problems, but only a few lines deal with the immediate concerns of testimonials and questionnaires. At the beginning of September E. Noether still intended to postpone accepting an invitation from Bryn Mawr College until 1934/35 because she believed she would be able to go to Oxford instead for the winter of 1933/34. At this time H. Weyl was on a lecture tour in the United States. On September 13, Emmy Noether wrote a post-

card to H. Hasse, "Today came the news of
the withdrawal of my venia* according to
§ 3, but the testimonials may still be of value
later on. Thanks again!" The rest of the message again concerns mathematics. By the end
of October, Emmy Noether was on her way
to America on board the "Bremen," to be a
visiting professor for one year.

* venia: right to teach

Bryn Mawr
and Princeton

(FALL 1933–SPRING 1935)

*I*N *PRINCETON*, New Jersey, Albert Einstein and Hermann Weyl had already been welcomed by Professor Veblen and Professor Flexner (1866–1959). The four of them did all they could to find or create positions for their European, especially their German, colleagues. This was by no means easy, and became more difficult as time went on. There were simply too many highly qualified people to be placed, especially Germans, and not enough universities which could afford to hire visiting professors. On the other hand, the responsibility of keeping all this talent from being wasted, of preventing mathematicians of genius from being forced into side lines or other professions, was certainly recognized. Committees for the support of emigrants were formed, some of them devoted to the task of clearing the path to legal immigration. A sponsor had to be found for each immigrant. The problems were many and complex. With what earnestness and sense of responsibility they were tackled, can be seen in Norbert Wiener's *I am a Mathematician* (Doubleday, Garden City, N.Y., 1956). A very revealing description of what went on in the mathematics departments of German and Austrian universities and technical colleges between 1933 and 1938 is found in the *Year Book of 1973* published by the Leo Baeck Institute in London, in an article by Max Pinl and Lux Furtmüller, entitled "Mathematicians under Hitler" (vol. XVIII, pp. 129–182). But perhaps the most immediate and shattering insight into this struggle is provided by the (unpublished) letters of Hermann Weyl. Better than any report intended for the public eye, these letters reveal the characters of the persons involved in this drama, and the suffering endured exactly by the best of them. It must not be assumed that the emigrants were satisfied to have escaped Nazi Germany and to have found a suitable place for themselves in free America. Most emigrants worried deeply about Germany and about the friends they had left behind, knowing how they suffered need or were in actual danger. This constant sorrow prevented them from enjoying their good fortune in having saved and even made secure their own lives and those of their families.

A position was found for Emmy Noether as a visiting professor at Bryn Mawr College.

Although this women's college had, and still has, an excellent reputation, anyone coming from Göttingen had to undergo an enormous adaptation, and without the warm congeniality with which she was received, and without her own self-sufficiency and capacity for adaptation to rely on, Emmy Noether would not have been able to assimilate the new circumstances as well as she did. At that time the mathematics department at Bryn Mawr was headed by Ann Pell Wheeler (1883–1966), who had studied in Göttingen in 1906 and 1907 and had obtained her doctor's degree in 1910 in Chicago. She and Emmy got on together very well. Mrs. Wheeler also met the numerous friends who came to visit Emmy from all over the world. While it is doubtful that Emmy Noether knew much about Bryn Mawr before she went there, certainly people at Bryn Mawr were aware of her and considered themselves fortunate to have her as a visitor. In the winter of 1933–34 Emmy Noether held a seminar with three "girls"—the word "student" was seldom used then—and one docent (or professor). Together they enthusiastically studied the first volume of van der Waerden's *Algebra,* and in between, the initial chapters of the *Theorie der algebraischen Zahlen* (Theory of algebraic numbers) by E. Hecke. The young women's enthusiasm and zeal was so great that they worked through all the problems in *Algebra I,*—which were, as Emmy stated in her report to Hasse, "certainly not assigned by me." In February 1934, Emmy Noether also began to give weekly lectures in nearby Princeton—not, as she wrote, at the "men's university where nothing female is admitted," but at the Flexner Institute which had only shortly before been established in 1930, on the initiative of A. Flexner and O. Veblen. It was an Institute for Advanced Study, the type of research establishment—long since proved useful—which allows scholars to pursue their research with the aid of stipends, free from obligations. Emmy Noether recognized that Princeton was striving to become as important as Göttingen, and was already approaching this goal in the number of professors, research fellows, so far. "In part, their standards in mathematics are already very good," she remarked to friends. Her own influence in determining the mathematical activity at Princeton is indicated in a letter to H. Hasse of March 6, 1934, "I have started with representation modules, groups with operators . . . ; Princeton will receive its first algebraic treatment this winter, and a thorough one at that." Then she told about H. Weyl, A. A. Albert (1905–1972), H. S. Vandiver (1882–1973) and John von Neumann and continued, "My audience consists mostly of research fellows, beside Albert and Vandiver, but I'm beginning to realize that I must be careful; after all, they are essentially used to explicit computation and I have already driven a few of them away with my approach! Between the University and the Flexner Institute, there are more than sixty professors and aspiring professors here."

In the summer of 1934 Emmy Noether went back to Germany once more, to see her brother Fritz (for the last time) before his emigration to Siberia, to visit old friends, and to break up her small household, having realized in the meantime that she would not return to Germany in the near future. She spent a few days in Hamburg with the Artins before she went to Göttingen. There she was given permission, as a "foreign scholar," to use the library. Apart from a few students, few of her friends and acquaintances were left. Hasse was still in Marburg, van der Waerden and Deuring in Leipzig. Emmy Noether attempted to help Deuring again and again, both from America and Göttingen. A letter she wrote in Göttingen, dated July 15, 1934, is entirely devoted to the subject of his desirable *Habilitation*. There is not a word about herself. Her brother, who had been *Ordinarius* in Breslau since 1922, had been forced into retirement for racial reasons, with a pension, before he was fifty years old. His older son was a student of chemistry; the younger one had passed the *Reifeprüfung* with honors in the spring of 1934 but the right to enroll at a university, to which this diploma entitles a person, was denied him. The only possibility left was emigration. A suitable position was available for Fritz Noether at the Research Institute for Mathematics and Mechanics of the University of Tomsk. The decision to emigrate to Siberia was not an easy one for him; he made it because it seemed to offer a chance for a decent future for his boys. For a few years all went well. Then the development of the political situation became fatal for a number of German scholars, among them Fritz Noether.

In the spring of 1934 Emmy left Europe again. Her future in America was secure at this point for only one more year, by an extension of her visiting professorship at Bryn Mawr. However, she had been sponsored, and her friends Veblen and Weyl in Princeton were prepared to use their influence to obtain a position for her as soon as necessary. She continued her work at Bryn Mawr optimistically and with undiminished enthusiasm. In the meantime, Richard Brauer (1901–1977) had also arrived in Princeton. On the scientific level Emmy Noether had been in close contact with him before; now exile strengthened the personal ties with him and his wife. After her lectures in Princeton she usually spent some time with Weyl, Veblen, and Brauer before returning to Bryn Mawr. On these weekly trips she was often accompanied by Olga Taussky, a young Austrian woman—today Professor Olga Taussky Todd of the California Institute of Technology—whom Emmy Noether had already known in Göttingen and whose talent she recognized and fostered. Olga was one of the three postgraduate women mathematicians at Bryn Mawr in 1934/35; the other two were Marie Weiss and Grace Shover (to become Grace Quinn; now at American University in Washington, D.C.). Olga was a specialist in number theory and had been a student of Philipp Furtwängler (1869–1940) in Vienna. She later developed independently of Noether's abstractionist influence. The following poem, which she composed while a student of Noether, might have amused Emmy if only Olga had not been too bashful to show it to her. It is a parody of a humorous poem by the German artist Wilhelm Busch (1832–1908) (*Es sitzt ein Vogel auf dem Leim*) and is quoted here, loosely translated.

Olga stands outside the class room
with wrinkled brow and in deep gloom.
Emmy, from far away comes along
with a firm step and feeling strong.

She climbs upstairs with a great swirl
and gets quite close to the poor girl.
Now Olga thinks: Of hope there is no ray
and Emmy scolds me anyway.
Merrily I will compute some more
and algebra I will ignore.
It makes me think that Olga had humor.

Translated
Dec. 1979   Olga Taussky Todd

Olga Taussky's colleague Marie Weiss, an algebraist who died young, wrote an article while still under E. Noether's influence, entitled, "Fundamental systems of units in normal fields." In addition to the three women who already had their doctor's degrees, there was Ruth Stauffer, E. Noether's only doctoral candidate at Bryn Mawr. These four women formed the core of the cheerful group centering around the great Göttingen algebraist. Ruth was writing her dissertation on "The construction of a normal basis in a separable normal extension field" (*Amer. Journ. Math.* 58, 585–597, 1936). Only one week before her death, E. Noether remarked that she would not be able to take her vacation before the end of June because it was her duty solemnly to confer the doctorate upon her pupil at commencement. In view of this, the sudden death of her motherly thesis advisor was especially painful for Ruth Stauffer. She took the examinations with R. Brauer instead, but eventually discontinued her scientific work altogether. Emmy Noether had held R. Stauffer in great esteem and probably would not have allowed her to abandon her mathematical work. It is with a sense of wistfulness that Ruth Stauffer—Mrs. McKee today—looks back on the good times she had at Bryn Mawr, and her modest, selfless professor whom she so admired, and who shared her time, her energy, and her great knowledge with all.

EMMY NOETHER'S last letter in Hasse's voluminous collection is dated April 7, 1935. It consists of two densely filled pages almost exclusively of mathematical content, concerning for the most part the theorems demonstrated in R. Stauffer's dissertation. There is not the slightest implication of any illness nor of an imminent operation. On April 15 Helmut Hasse, chairman of the DMV, received the following message from Fritz Noether in Berlin:

Dear Colleague,

I am informed by cablegram that my sister Emmy Noether died in Bryn Mawr, Pennsylvania following a surgical operation. No further details are known to me at this point, but I assume that her illness was very brief since even most recently her regular correspondence gave no indication of it.

Since I myself am only here temporarily and will return to Russia in the immediate future, I must restrict myself to this brief message for now.

With greetings from your colleague,
Yours truly,

Noether
(Tomsk, Forsch. Inst. f. Math. und Mech.)

P.S. The cremation and funeral ceremonies will be held in Bryn Mawr.

On Monday, April 15, 1935, in the third column of page 19 of the *New York Times*, attentive readers may have spotted the following little notice:

Dr. Emmy Noether, visiting Professor of Mathematics at Bryn Mawr College, died today in a hospital where she underwent an operation last week. She was 52 years old. Dr. Noether formerly taught mathematics at the University of Goettingen in Germany. She came to this country two years ago.

On the same page, in the alphabetical listing of deaths, an even briefer notice states that the hospital concerned was the Bryn Mawr Hospital.

On the same day, the *New York Herald*

Tribune printed the following notice on page 12:

Dr. Emmy Noether Dies
Noted as Mathematician

*Bryn Mawr College Professor
Was Nazi Exile*

SPECIAL TO THE HERALD TRIBUNE.

Bryn Mawr, Pa. April 14.—Dr. Emmy Noether, exiled German teacher, considered one of the greatest women mathematicians of the world, died here today in Bryn Mawr Hospital. She was fifty-two years old.

Dr. Noether had been teaching mathematics in Bryn Mawr College since her exile from Germany, where she was born. Dr. Noether entered Erlangen University, where her father was a professor of mathematics, after completing her early education. After receiving a doctor of philosophy degree, she became an instructor of mathematics at the University of Goettingen, Germany.

Dr. Noether suffered anti-Semitic persecution when the Nazis came into power. She left Germany two years ago to come to the United States. Soon after her arrival here Dr. Noether was invited to become associated with the department of mathematics at Bryn Mawr College. She also lectured before the research institute at Princeton University.

A brother, Dr. Fritz Noether, who teaches mathematical physics in a university in Russia, survives.

In his great memorial address, Hermann Weyl described the circumstances of Emmy Noether's death with the words, "She seemed to have got well over an operation for tumor; we thought her to be on the way to convalescence when an unexpected complication led her suddenly on the downward path to her death within a few hours."

THE CREMATION of the body took place in Bryn Mawr. A small group of friends of the deceased, both from her first and her second home, each took leave of her with a few words, spoken in their respective native tongues—Herman Weyl, Richard Brauer, Olga Taussky, Ann Pell Wheeler. The urn containing the ashes was placed in the Library Cloister of Bryn Mawr College. On April 19, S. Lefschetz announced Emmy Noether's death to the American Mathematical Society in a meeting at Columbia University in New York. All honored the memory of their dead colleague by standing for one minute of silence. On April 26 a memorial service was held in Goodhart Hall, the last scene of E. Noether's professional activity, a large number of people attending. Hermann Weyl came from Princeton to give his remarkable memorial address in English (list of obituaries #6).* Printed copies of it were dis-

* See Appendix B.

tributed among E. Noether's absent friends after the war, when it became possible again to contact those who had remained in Germany, or who had returned there. These copies included the same photograph of Emmy Noether as that reproduced in the mural display mentioned in the beginning of this biography. It also appears in books such as *Gelöste und ungelöste mathematische Probleme aus alter und neuer Zeit* (Solved and unsolved mathematical problems in modern and premodern times) by H. Tietze (Munich, 1964) (bearing Emmy Noether's characteristic signature), or *Kleine Enzyklopädie* (Zurich-Vienna 1966), where it appears in the company of such good friends as Erhard Schmidt, Constantin Carathéodory, David Hilbert, and Dedekind. Only one page earlier in this book we find a portrait of the other great woman mathematician of modern times, Sonia Kovalevsky (1850–1891), who is often mentioned in the same breath with Emmy Noether and is sometimes compared with her. The two portraits are in striking contrast. Yet no matter how different people may compare these two personalities as to their looks and character, when it comes to the magnitude of their creative achievement there tends to be agreement that Emmy Noether was not equalled or surpassed by any woman mathematician, not even by Sonia Kovalevsky. Her conceptual and repre-

sentative abilities and her unusually powerful tendency to abstract place Emmy Noether
"in the first row of a whole phalanx of algebraists of world-wide renown." (Obituary
#5).*

ON JUNE 21, 1935 the obituary by B. L. van
der Waerden was received by the editors of
the *Mathematische Annalen*. In its concise
form, it does justice to Emmy Noether's
mathematical mind. On September 26, 1935,
in an administrative session held on the occasion of the annual meeting of the DMV,
Emmy Noether was named by the secretary
as one of the fourteen members who had
died during the past year. The assembly rose
from their seats to honor their dead. That is
all that is mentioned in the annual report of
the DMV. The only consequence was that
Emmy Noether's name was absent from the
list of members from then on. But it did not
disappear from mathematical literature. Before mathematical research in Europe came
to an almost total standstill in the course of
the war, algebraic work was still being done
in places, and papers from the Noether school
were naturally used and quoted. It is true
that a few extremists tried to divide mathematics into Jewish and Aryan, but that division was not recognized by the majority of
mathematicians.

* See Appendix B.

Van der Waerden's obituary is the only one existing in the German language. Of the seven others, the one by Weyl is the most comprehensive, and the one which succeeds best in expressing Emmy Noether as a human being. The obituary by Kořínek (#7) is also written with much sympathy and factual knowledge. Albert Einstein's commentary in the *New York Times* of May 5, 1935 honors him as it does Emmy Noether. It deserves to be quoted here:

THE LATE EMMY NOETHER.

Professor Einstein Writes in
Appreciation of a Fellow-Mathematician.

To the Editor of The New York Times:
  The efforts of most human beings are consumed in the struggle for their daily bread, but most of those who are, either through fortune or some special gift, relieved of this struggle are largely absorbed in further improving their worldly lot. Beneath the effort directed toward the accumulation of worldly goods lies all too frequently the illusion that this is the most substantial and desirable end to be achieved; but there is, fortunately, a minority composed of those who recognize early in their lives that the most beautiful and satisfying experiences open to humankind are not derived from the outside, but are bound up with the development of the individual's own feeling, thinking and acting. The genuine artists, investigators and thinkers

have always been persons of this kind. However inconspicuously the life of these individuals runs its course, none the less the fruits of their endeavors are the most valuable contributions which one generation can make to its successors.

Within the past few days a distinguished mathematician, Professor Emmy Noether, formerly connected with the University of Göttingen and for the past two years at Bryn Mawr College, died in her fifty-third year. In the judgment of the most competent living mathematicians, Fraeulein Noether was the most significant creative mathematical genius thus far produced since the higher education of women began. In the realm of algebra, in which the most gifted mathematicians have been busy for centuries, she discovered methods which have proved of enormous importance in the development of the present-day younger generation of mathematicians. Pure mathematics is, in its way, the poetry of logical ideas. One seeks the most general ideas of operation which will bring together in simple, logical and unified form the largest possible circle of formal relationships. In this effort toward logical beauty spiritual formulas are discovered necessary for the deeper penetration into the laws of nature.

Born in a Jewish family distinguished for the love of learning, Emmy Noether, who, in spite of the efforts of the great Goettingen mathematician, Hilbert, never reached the academic standing due her in her own country, none the less surrounded herself with a group

93

of students and investigators at Goettingen, who have already become distinguished as teachers and investigators. Her unselfish, significant work over a period of many years was rewarded by the new rulers of Germany with a dismissal, which cost her the means of maintaining her simple life and the opportunity to carry on her mathematical studies. Farsighted friends of science in this country were fortunately able to make such arrangements at Bryn Mawr College and at Princeton that she found in America up to the day of her death not only colleagues who esteemed her friendship but grateful pupils whose enthusiasm made her last years the happiest and perhaps the most fruitful of her entire career.

ALBERT EINSTEIN.
Princeton University, May 1, 1935.

Lastly, the conclusion of the rather poetic obituary #5* from South America may be quoted here, "The veneration which the intellect of this admirable woman generates is no less ardent than the reverence and love she inspires in her students by her personal qualities. This may be a lesson to those who still today follow the medieval practice of judging women as intellectually and psychologically inferior."

AFTER THE most difficult years of the first postwar period scientific activity in Germany

* See Appendix B.

gradually returned to normal. Many emigrants came back, among them friends of Emmy Noether. International exchange became possible again, and all periodicals accessible to anyone. Today, many people in America, Europe, USSR, and Japan continue to work in abstract algebra in the spirit of the Göttingen school—perhaps only rarely remembering the woman who helped initiate this direction of thought.

In most reference books the Noethers used to be listed first under Max, with Emmy being described as "daughter of Max N." Today the list reads, "Max N., father of Emmy N.," and more space is allocated for Emmy than for her father; in some books she is the only Noether listed. Fritz Noether is always referred to as "brother of Emmy N." Gottfried Noether, professor of mathematical statistics, is referred to socially, as a matter of course, as the "nephew of Emmy N."—all of which proves that Landau's statement about Emmy being the origin of coordinates of the Noether family was justified.

Although the memory of Emmy Noether is kept alive by the continuation of her work rather than by memorial events, those which occurred should be mentioned here. The commemoration of Emmy's seventieth birthday in Berlin was already referred to on p. 52. A report of this event, with special attention to the speech by Heinrich Grell, appeared on

May 15, 1952 in *Forum*, a journal about the intellectual life at German universities. The University of Erlangen celebrated the golden anniversary of Emmy Noether's doctoral graduation in 1957. In 1960, the town of Erlangen decided to name the streets of a newly developed residential district in Bruck after eminent natural scientists and mathematicians. Thus, a street running parallel to Heinrich Hertz Street became Noether Street (*Noetherstrasse*). The population registry of 1962 informs us that this street was "named after the two Erlangen mathematicians Max N. and his daughter Emmi N." The initial idea for naming it thus came from Dr. Otto Haupt, professor emeritus at the University of Erlangen. He suggested the names of several mathematicians, but pointed out that if not all of them could be considered, Emmy Noether's ought to be the first choice. The *Erlanger Tagblatt* used the occasion of this naming to revive the memory of the Noethers with a picture of Max and an article on the lives and professional achievements of both Max and his daughter (number 149, July 1/2, 1961). In 1967 the town of Erlangen celebrated its six-hundredth birthday. In its celebration issue the *Erlanger Tagblatt* published an article entitled, *"Die erste Doktorandin: eine mathematische Kapazität"* (The first woman to receive the doctor's degree, a prominent mathematician). Its author, Mrs.

Ilse Sponsel, offered to the general public whatever information she had been able to accumulate on the period when women were first allowed to enter academic careers, and on Emmy Noether's Erlangen period, thereby recalling Erlangen's most illustrious daughter to nonmathematicians as well. The same article appeared, slightly changed, in the annual report (1966/67) of the *Städtisches Marie-Therese-Gymnasium*, the institution which succeeded the same school in which Emmy Noether had spent eight years. In March 1978, *Das neue Erlangen*, a periodical on science, economics, and culture, published another essay by the same author, on the occasion of the 70th anniversary of the doctoral examinations taken by the first woman candidate from Erlangen, Emmy Noether.

It has been mentioned on p. 55 of this biography that the terms Fitting's lemma and Fitting's radical were derived from the name of one of Noether's pupils. It goes without saying that the name of the master algebraist herself was used also to characterize concepts specific to abstract algebra as they evolved through the continuation of Noether's work, particularly in the area of the theory of rings and of groups. Thus, a ring is called Noetherian if each ideal has a finite basis. A group is called Noetherian if each subgroup can be generated by a finite basis. In addition, we speak of Noetherian equations, Noetherian modules,

Noetherian factor systems, etc. The book by Lesieur and Croisot uses the attribute "Noetherian" in its title. So does the book *Simple Noetherian Rings* by John Cozzens and C. C. Falth (Cambridge University Press, 1975). The value of such designations might be argued, of course, but it seems reasonable to assume that they express respect and admiration for the bearer of that name, and the wish to preserve the memory of the person among those who work with these terms.

In the first year of Emmy Noether's activity at Bryn Mawr College a scholarship fund was already established for post-graduate women mathematicians, called the Emmy Noether Fellowship, to be drawn from at intervals of several years. Emmy was delighted by this since the promotion of talented young people had always been of vital concern to her. With so many students having received a stipend thanks to her mediation, it is really very gratifying that her memory lives on in the name of such a foundation in the U.S.

Naturally, only a relatively small group of people work with abstract algebra or even understand or attempt to understand it. For the others, Emmy Noether is of interest simply as a person standing out among others. She stands out not only among women but among algebraists, even among exceptional ones. As was the case with many of her contemporaries, her fate was in part determined by her Jewish origin; many had to endure the predicament of an emigrant scholar, as she did; but few succeeded in making of that situation what she made of it.

As part of the program *Um uns die Fremde* ("About us, homelessness") jointly sponsored by German Television, the station *Freies Berlin* broadcast a documentary on April 30, 1967, called *Die Wissenschaftler im Exil* (Scientists in exile). It was pointed out in the program that the percentage loss of scholars suffered by the German universities in 1933 was greatest for mathematicians. Pictures from the mathematical Institute in Göttingen were shown. Richard Courant was interviewed at the Institute at New York University which is named after him. While he was talking about the spring of 1933 and the dissolution of the faculty of mathematics and the natural sciences soon thereafter, the portrait of Emmy Noether appeared on the screen. It may have surprised some of the people watching the show; others will have understood it to mean that Emmy Noether was an important scholar who will be remembered by future generations.

Obituary of
*Emmy Noether**

by B. L. van der Waerden, Leipzig

Our science has suffered a tragic loss. On April 14, 1935, Emmy Noether, our devoted collaborator at the *Mathematische Annalen* for many years, a highly unique person, and a scientist of great importance, died following a surgical operation. She was born in Erlangen on March 23, 1882, the daughter of the well-known mathematician Max Noether.

Her originality, absolute beyond comparison, was not a matter of her bearing, characteristic though this was. Nor did it exhaust itself in the fact that this highly gifted mathematician was a woman. Rather, it lay in the fundamental structure of her creative mind, in the mode of her thinking, and in the aim of her endeavors. Since the form of her thinking was primarily mathematical, and her aim was directed specifically towards scientific insight, it is necessary to analyze her

* Published in *Mathematische Annalen* 111 (1935), pp. 469–474. The list of publications originally included with the obituary (p. 475) has been omitted here; a comparable list appears on page 187 of the present volume.

mathematical work in order to gain an understanding of her personality.

The maxim by which Emmy Noether was guided throughout her work might be formulated as follows: "Any relationships between numbers, functions and operations only become transparent, generally applicable, and fully productive after they have been isolated from their particular objects and been formulated as universally valid concepts."

Emmy Noether did not arrive at this principle as a result of her experience with the significance of scientific methods—rather, it was an a priori principle, fundamental to her thinking. She was unable to grasp any theorem, any argument unless it had been made abstract and thus made transparent to the eye of her mind. She could only think in concepts, not in formulas, and precisely here lay her strength. It was the very nature of her mind which compelled her to invent conceptual forms which were suitable as carriers for mathematical theories.

The material which readily lent itself to her method of thinking was algebra and arithmetic. She recognized as basic the concepts of field, ring, ideal, module, residue class and isomorphism. She found a primary model for the development of her conceptualizations in Dedekind's theory of modules from which she was able to extricate new ideas and methods again and again, thereby expanding the range of its application amazingly in every direction.

She started out with Gordan's theory of invariants. Her doctoral dissertation (2)* of 1907 in Erlangen deals with the problem of transferring the methods developed by Gordan for binary and ternary forms to n-ary forms. The n-ary expansions found beautiful applications in her later research (8), (16).

Very soon, however, she began to be fascinated by Hilbert's methods and the direction of his research. Her proofs of finiteness for invariants of finite groups (7) and for integral invariants of binary forms belong to Hilbert's area of research. Her most important work from that period is that on fields and systems of rational functions (6) in which she combines the methods of Hilbert's proofs of finiteness with those of Steinitz's field theory to demonstrate the existence of a rational basis for each system of rational functions of n variables. On the basis of this she was able to solve part of Hilbert's problem of relative entire functions. By the same methods as those used in this paper (6) she later also achieved an essential contribution—the most significant made by anyone so far—to the problem of constructing equations having a prescribed Galois group (11).

---

*The numbers refer to the list of publications in Appendix A.

During the war Emmy Noether came to Göttingen where she was *habilitiert* in 1919 and soon thereafter obtained a teaching position. Under the influence of Klein and Hilbert, who during that time were both deeply involved with the general theory of relativity, she produced her papers on differential invariants (12, 13) which became fundamentally important in this field. These papers demonstrate, for the first time, the general methods by which all differential invariants may be generated. The first work establishes the fundamental concept of the system of reduction—a system of differential invariants in relation to which all remaining ones are algebraic invariants. The second work uses the methods of the formal calculus of variations to produce differential invariants.

Through the study of the arithmetical theory of algebraic functions (14), Emmy Noether became familiar with Dedekind's theory of modules and ideals, which helped to determine the direction of her further work. In the paper she produced in collaboration with Schmeidler (17), concepts from the theory of modules—direct sums and intersections, residue class modules, isomorphy of modules—are developed and tried; they appear like a red thread throughout her later work. In this paper, also, uniqueness proofs are given for the first time by means of the method of exchange, and the representation of modules as intersections is achieved by means of a finiteness condition.

The first major success of this method was achieved in 1921 in the paper, *Idealtheorie in Ringbereichen* (19), which has become a classic. Following a definition of the terms "ring" and "ideal," a finiteness condition—the ascending chain condition—is shown to be equivalent to Hilbert's theorem of the finite ideal basis. The representation of ideals as intersections of primary ideals—formerly obtained by E. Lasker with the aid of the theory of ideals for the polynomial domain—is shown to be a consequence of the ascending chain condition alone. In addition to the concept of a primary ideal (which is an abstract form of Lasker's concept and at the same time a generalization of Dedekind's concept of an *einartiges* ideal), the concept of the irreducible ideal is established, and four uniqueness theorems are proved by the module-theoretic methods as mentioned above.

This work forms the immovable foundation of today's "general theory of ideals." The results called for elaboration in two directions. First, the theory of elimination had to be incorporated into the general theory of ideals, and the theory of zeros of polynomial ideals had to be reconsidered from the new point of view. Emmy Noether wrestled with this problem in her paper on Hentzelt's theory of elimination (22) and in two further papers (25 and 24), but it was only in her lectures of 1923/24 that she arrived at the solution in its final form. It is a testament to her generosity that, a year later, when on the basis of her papers I had arrived at the same proof of the theory of zeros, she left the publication of the results to me.

The second task was to establish the connection between the general theory of ideals and Dedekind's classical theory of ideals for the rings of integers in algebraic number fields and function fields. It was a matter of determining the requirements a ring must meet in order for every ideal to become not only an intersection of primary ideals but equally a product of powers of prime ideals. This problem, too, was solved completely (30). It was found that besides the finiteness conditions (ascending chain condition and *Vielfachenkettensatz*) the condition of the ring being integrally closed was essential. By transferring the conditions of finiteness to finite extensions of a ring, Emmy Noether arrived at the same time, by her earlier method of the theory of invariants, at a theorem of finiteness for modular invariants (29).

Her great papers centered around the theory of ideals (19 and 30) spawned a long series of highly productive efforts, mostly by students of hers. W. Krull has given a summary description of these in his report

Idealtheorie (*Ergebnisse der Mathematik*, 4, 3, 1935).

In the meantime, Emmy Noether herself had become involved with another complex of problems. The same module-theoretic concepts from which she had developed her commutative theory of ideals were to prove their strength in a noncommutative context as well. The first result was the successful incorporation of the theory of representation for groups and hypercomplex systems into the theory of modules. For every representation of a system R by linear transformations there is a unique R-module, the "module of representation." With that, the concept of equivalence in the theory of representation is easily subjected to the concept of module isomorphism, and the terms "reducible," "irreducible" and "completely reducible" turn out to be special cases of notions from the theory of modules. Thus the following theorem central to the theory of representation crystallizes: Every irreducible R-module is equivalent to an ideal of the ring R.

This close connection between the theories of representation, of modules, and of ideals had already been developed by Emmy Noether in her lectures in 1924 (cf. 28). It is also fundamental to her paper on discriminants (31). But it only was fully clarified and generalized in her lectures of 1927/28 in Göttingen and in the resultant paper (34). This paper also contains a systematic theory of ideals for hypercomplex systems which culminates in this theorem: The semi-simple hypercomplex systems as conceived by J. H. Maclagan-Wedderburn are the direct sums of simple right ideals; their representations are also fully reducible. From this insight the entire theory of representations as devised from Frobenius was developed and even generalized. For, while Frobenius' theory proceeded from the field of complex numbers, Noether's theory made it possible to approach representations in any field directly. Now arose the question of the relationships between the representations in different fields (called the arithmetical theory of groups of linear substitutions), and in particular the question of the splitting fields in which a prescribed representation consists of absolutely irreducible ones. In Noether's theory these questions are contained in the more general question of the structure of the product of two simple hypercomplex systems, a question which she answered exhaustively by using the methods of module theory (40). Above all, this process produced a characterization of the splitting fields of a division algebra as maximal commutative subfields of the algebra itself or of a full matrix ring over this algebra (32). This imbedding of the splitting fields at the same time provides deep insight into the structure of the algebra itself. It can be interpreted as "crossed product" of the splitting field with its Galois group.*

The simplest case of the crossed product is the "cyclic algebra" which occurs when the splitting field is cyclic and imbedded in the algebra itself. The structure of such a cyclic algebra depends on whether or not certain elements of the ground field are norms of elements of the splitting field. If the ground field is an algebraic number field, then the theory of norms of cyclic expansions becomes an object to class field theory which in this instance is revealed as closely related to the theory of algebras (39). Further exploitation of this connection by Noether, H. Hasse, R. Brauer and C. Chevalley—who all mutually influenced each other—led on the one hand to a refoundation of certain parts of class field theory by hypercomplex methods, and on the other hand to the proof of a "principal theorem in the theory of algebras," long assumed to be true, which says that every division algebra over an algebraic number field is cyclic (38).

The consideration of crossed products in place of cyclic algebras allowed the extension of theorems of class field theory, in particular

* Emmy Noether's theory of crossed products is explained by H. Hasse in "Theory of cyclic algebras", *Trans. Amer. Math. Soc.* 34, p. 180–200, as well as in M. Deuring's report "Algebren", *Ergebn. Math. 4*, 1, p. 52–56.

of the *"Hauptgeschlechtssatz"*, to nonabelian fields (41).

With her conceptual penetration of class field theory Emmy Noether had reached a goal she had been consistently striving towards for many years, undeterred by the doubts voiced by number theorists. The attainment of this goal, however, by no means meant the end of her research. Untiringly, and in spite of unfavorable external circumstances, she pursued the path indicated by the concepts she had created. When she lost permission to teach in Göttingen in 1933 and was appointed by the Women's College of Bryn Mawr (Pennsylvania), she succeeded in gathering again a school around herself within a short time, both at Bryn Mawr and in nearby Princeton. Her research, which had passed through the fields of commutative algebra, commutative arithmetics, and non-commutative algebra, now turned to noncommutative arithmetics (42) but was abruptly terminated by her death.

These we have found to be her outstanding characteristics: a powerful ability to strive with incredible energy and consistency towards conceptual penetration of her subject matter, with the aim of achieving utmost methodical clarity; a tenacious insistence on methods and concepts she had found to be valuable, no matter how abstract and unproductive they might appear to her contemporaries; a marked proclivity to place specific cases within general conceptual schemes.

In a number of respects, her thinking indeed does differ from that of most other mathematicians. All of us like to rely on figures and formulas. For her, these tools were worthless—in fact, obstructing. She was concerned with concepts only, not with visualization or calculation. The Gothic letters which she was in the habit of throwing on the blackboard or paper in typically simplified form represented concepts to her rather than objects of a more or less mechanical computation.

This entirely non-visual and noncalculative mind of hers was probably one of the main reasons why her lectures were difficult to follow. She was without didactic talent, and the touching efforts she made to clarify her statements, even before she had finished pronouncing them, by rapidly adding explanations, tended to produce the opposite effect. And yet, how profound the impact of her lecturing was! Her small, loyal audience, usually consisting of a few advanced students and often of an equal number of professors and guests, had to strain enormously in order to follow her. Yet those who succeeded gained far more than they would have from the most polished lecture. She almost never presented completed theories; usually they were in the process of being developed. Each of her lectures was a program. And no one was happier than she herself when this program was carried out by her students. Entirely free of egotism and vanity she never asked anything for herself but first of all fostered the work of her students. She always wrote the introductions to our papers, formulating for us the principal ideas which we, as beginners, could never have grasped and pronounced with her clarity. She was both a loyal friend and a severe critic. It is these qualities which made her so valuable an editor, too, for the *Mathematische Annalen*.

As already mentioned, her abstract, non-visual conceptualizations met with little recognition at first. This changed as the productivity of her methods was gradually perceived even by those who did not agree with them. During her last eight years in Göttingen, prominent mathematicians from all over Germany as well as abroad came to consult with her and attend her lectures. In 1932, together with E. Artin, she received the Ackermann-Teubner memorial award for arithmetics and algebra. And today, carried by the strength of her thought, modern algebra appears to be well on its way to victory in every part of the civilized world.

*Emmy Noether**
by Hermann Weyl

With deep dismay Emmy Noether's friends living in America learned about her sudden passing away on Sunday, April 14. She seemed to have got well over an operation for tumor; we thought her to be on the way to convalescence when an unexpected complication led her suddenly on the downward path to her death within a few hours. She was such a paragon of vitality, she stood on the earth so firm and healthy with a certain sturdy humor and courage for life, that nobody was prepared for this eventuality. She was at the summit of her mathematical creative power; her far-reaching imagination and her technical abilities accumulated by continued experience, had come to a perfect balance; she had eagerly set to work on new problems. And now suddenly—the end, her voice silenced, her work abruptly broken off.

* Memorial Address delivered in Goodhart Hall, Bryn Mawr College, on April 26, 1935. Published in *Scripta mathematica* III, 3 (1935), pp. 201–220

Down, down, down into the darkness of the
grave
Gently they go, the beautiful, the tender, the
kind;
Quietly they go, the intelligent, the witty, the
brave.
I know. But I do not approve. And I am not
resigned.

A mood of defiance similar to that expressed in this "Dirge without music" by
Edna St. Vincent Millay, mingles with our
mourning in the present hour when we are
gathered to commemorate our friend, her life
and work and personality.

I am not able to tell much about the out-
ward story of her life; far from her home and
those places where she lived and worked in
the continuity of decades, the necessary information could not be secured. She was
born the 23d of March, 1882, in the small
South German university town of Erlangen.
Her father was Max Noether, himself a great
mathematician who played an important
rôle in the development of the theory of
algebraic functions as the chief representative
of the algebraic-geometric school. He had
come to the University of Erlangen as a professor of mathematics in 1875, and stayed
there until his death in 1921. Besides Emmy
there grew up in the house her brother Fritz,
younger by two and a half years. He turned
to applied mathematics in later years, was

until recently professor at the Technische Hochschule in Breslau, and by the same fate that ended Emmy's career in Göttingen is now driven off to the Research Institute for Mathematics and Mechanics in Tomsk, Siberia. The Noether family is a striking example of the hereditary nature of the mathematical talent, the most shining illustration of which is the Basle Huguenot dynasty of the Bernoullis.

Side by side with Noether acted in Erlangen as a mathematician the closely befriended Gordan, an offspring of Clebsch's school like Noether himself. Gordan had come to Erlangen shortly before, in 1874, and he, too, remained associated with that university until his death in 1912. Emmy wrote her doctor's thesis under him in 1907: "On complete systems of invariants for ternary biquadratic forms"; it is entirely in line with the Gordan spirit and his problems. The *Mathematische Annalen* contains a detailed obituary of Gordan and an analysis of his work, written by Max Noether with Emmy's collaboration. Besides her father, Gordan must have been well-nigh one of the most familiar figures in Emmy's early life, first as a friend of the house, later as a mathematician also; she kept a profound reverence for him though her own mathematical taste soon developed in quite a different direction. I remember that his picture decorated the wall of her study in Göttingen. These two men, the father and Gordan, determined the atmosphere in which she grew up. Therefore I shall venture to describe them with a few strokes.

Riemann had developed the theory of algebraic functions of one variable and their integrals, the so-called Abelian integrals, by a function-theoretic transcendental method resting on the minimum principle of potential theory which he named after Dirichlet, and had uncovered the purely topological foundations of the manifold function-theoretic relations governing this domain. (Stringent proof of Dirichlet's principle which seemed so evident from the physicist's standpoint was only given about fifty years later by Hilbert.) There remained the task of replacing and securing his transcendental existential proofs by the explicit algebraic construction starting with the equation of the algebraic curve. Weierstrass solved this problem (in his lectures published in detail only later) in his own half function-theoretic, half algebraic way, but Clebsch had introduced Riemann's ideas into the geometric theory of algebraic curves and Noether became, after Clebsch had passed away young, his executor in this matter: he succeeded in erecting the whole structure of the algebraic geometry of curves on the basis of the so-called Noether residual theorem. This line of research was taken up later on, mainly in Italy; the vein Noether struck is still a profusely gushing spring of investigations; among us, men like Lefschetz and Zariski bear witness thereto. Later on there arose, beside Riemann's transcendental and Noether's algebraic-geometric method, an arithmetical theory of algebraic functions due to Dedekind and Weber on the one side, to Hensel and Landsberg on the other. Emmy Noether stood closer to this trend of thought. A brief report on the arithmetical theory of algebraic functions that parallels the corresponding notions in the competing theories was published by her in 1920 in the Jahresberichte der Deutschen Mathematikervereinigung. She thus supplemented the well-known report by Brill and her father on the algebraic-geometric theory that had appeared in 1894 in one of the first volumes of the Jahresberichte. Noether's residual theorem was later fitted by Emmy into her general theory of ideals in arbitrary rings. This scientific kinship of father and daughter—who became in a certain sense his successor in algebra, but stands beside him independent in her fundamental attitude and in her problems—is something extremely beautiful and gratifying. The father was—such is the impression I gather from his papers and even more from the many obituary biographies he wrote for the *Mathematische Annalen*—a very intelligent, warm-hearted harmonious man of many-sided interests and sterling education.

Gordan was of a different stamp. A queer fellow, impulsive and one-sided. A great walker and talker—he liked that kind of walk to which frequent stops at a beer-garden or a café belong. Either with friends, and then accompanying his discussions with violent gesticulations, completely irrespective of his surroundings; or alone, and then murmuring to himself and pondering over mathematical problems; or if in an idler mood, carrying out long numerical calculations by heart. There always remained something of the eternal "Bursche" of the 1848 type about him—an air of dressing gown, beer and tobacco, relieved however by a keen sense of humor and a strong dash of wit. When he had to listen to others, in classrooms or at meetings, he was always half asleep. As a mathematician not of Noether's rank, and of an essentially different kind. Noether himself concludes his characterization of him with the short sentence: "Er war ein Algorithmiker." His strength rested on the invention and calculative execution of formal processes. There exist papers of his where twenty pages of formulas are not interrupted by a single text word; it is told that in all his papers he himself wrote the formulas only, the text being added by his friends. Noether says of him:

"The formula always and everywhere was the indispensable support for the formation of his thoughts, his conclusions and his mode of expression. . . . In his lectures he carefully avoided any fundamental definition of conceptual kind, even that of the limit."

He, too, had belonged to Clebsch's most intimate collaborators, had written with Clebsch their book on Abelian integrals; he later shifted over to the theory of invariants following his formal talent; here he added considerably to the development of the so-called symbolic method, and he finally succeeded in proving by means of this computative method of explicit construction the finiteness of a rational integral basis for binary invariants. Years later Hilbert demonstrated the theorem much more generally for an arbitrary number of variables—by an entirely new approach, the characteristic Hilbertian species of methods, putting aside the whole apparatus of symbolic treatment and attacking the thing itself as directly as possible. *Ex ungue leonem*—the young lion Hilbert showed his claws. It was, however, at first only an existential proof providing for no actual finite algebraic construction. Hence Gordan's characteristic exclamation: "This is not mathematics, but theology!" What then would he have said about his former pupil Emmy Noether's later "theology", that abhorred all calculation and operated in a much thinner air of abstraction than Hilbert ever dared!

Gordan once struck upon a formal analogy between binary invariants and the scheme of valence bonds in chemistry—the same analogy by which Sylvester had been surprised many years before when thinking about an illustration of invariant theory appropriate for an audience of laymen; it is the subject of Sylvester's paper in the first volume of the *American Journal of Mathematics* founded by him at Johns Hopkins. Gordan seems to have been unaware of his predecessor. Anyway, he was led by his little discovery to propose the establishment of chairs for a new science, "mathematical chemistry", all over the German universities; I mention this as an incident showing his impetuosity and lack of survey. By the way, modern quantum mechanics recently has changed this analogy into a true theory disclosing the binary invariants as the mathematical tool for describing the several valence states of a molecule in spin space.

The meteor Felix Klein, whose mathematical genius caught fire through the collision of Riemann's and Galois' worlds of ideas, skimmed Erlangen before Emmy was born; he promulgated there his "Erlanger Programm", but soon moved on to Munich. By him Gordan was inspired to those invariant theoretical investigations that center around

Klein's book on the icosahedron and the adjoint questions in the theory of algebraic equations. Even after their local separation both continued in their intense cooperation—a queer contrasting team if one comes to think of Gordan's formal type and Klein's, entirely oriented by intuition. The general problem at the bottom of their endeavors, Klein's form problem has likewise stayed alive to our days and quite recently has undergone a new deep-reaching treatment by Dr. Brauer's applying to it the methods of hypercomplex number systems and their representations which formed the main field of Emmy Noether's activities during the last six or seven years.

It is queer enough that a formalist like Gordan was the mathematician from whom her mathematical orbit set out; a greater contrast is hardly imaginable than between her first paper, the dissertation, and her works of maturity; for the former is an extreme example of formal computations and the latter constitute an extreme and grandiose example of conceptual axiomatic thinking in mathematics. Her thesis ends with a table of the complete system of covariant forms for a given ternary quartic consisting of not less than 331 forms in symbolic representation. It is an awe-inspiring piece of work; but today I am afraid we should be inclined to rank it among those achievements with regard to which Gordan himself once said when asked about the use of the theory of invariants: "Oh, it is very useful indeed; one can write many theses about it."

It is not quite easy to evoke before an American audience a true picture of that state of German life in which Emmy Noether grew up in Erlangen; maybe the present generation in Germany is still more remote from it. The great stability of burgher life was in her case accentuated by the fact that Noether (and Gordan too) were settled at one university for so long an uninterrupted period. One may dare to add that the time of the primary proper impulses of their production was gone, though they undoubtedly continued to be productive mathematicians; in this regard, too, the atmosphere around her was certainly tinged by a quiet uniformity. Moreover, there belongs to the picture the high standing, and the great solidity in the recognition of, spiritual values; based on a solid education, a deep and genuine active interest in the higher achievements of intellectual culture, and on a well-developed faculty of enjoying them. There must have prevailed in the Noether home a particularly warm and companionable family life. Emmy Noether herself was, if I may say so, warm like a loaf of bread. There irradiated from her a broad, comforting, vital warmth. Our generation accuses that time of lacking all moral sincerity, of hiding behind its comfort and bourgeois peacefulness, and of ignoring the profound creative and terrible forces that really shape man's destiny; moreover of shutting its eyes to the contrast between the spirit of true Christianity which was confessed, and the private and public life as it was actually lived. Nietzsche arose in Germany as a great awakener. It is hardly possible to exaggerate the significance which Nietzsche (whom by the way Noether once met in the Engadin) had in Germany for the thorough change in the moral and mental atmosphere. I think he was fundamentally right—and yet one should not deny that in wide circles in Germany, as with the Noethers, the esteem in which the spiritual goods were held, the intellectual culture, good-heartedness, and human warmth were thoroughly genuine—notwithstanding their sentimentality, their Wagnerianism, and their plush sofas.

Emmy Noether took part in the housework as a young girl, dusted and cooked, and went to dances, and it seems her life would have been that of an ordinary woman had it not happened that just about that time it became possible in Germany for a girl to enter on a scientific career without meeting any too marked resistance. There was nothing rebellious in her nature; she was willing to accept conditions as they were. But now she became a mathematician. Her dependence on Gordan did not last long; he was important as a starting point, but was not of lasting scientific influence upon her. Nevertheless the Erlangen mathematical air may have been responsible for making her into an algebraist. Gordan retired in 1910; he was followed first by Erhard Schmidt, and the next year by Ernst Fischer. Fischer's field was algebra again, in particular the theory of elimination and of invariants. He exerted upon Emmy Noether, I believe, a more penetrating influence than Gordan did. Under his direction the transition from Gordan's formal standpoint to the Hilbert method of approach was accomplished. She refers in her papers at this time again and again to conversations with Fischer. This epoch extends until about 1919. The main interest is concentrated on finite rational and integral bases; the proof of finiteness is given by her for the invariants of a finite group (without using Hilbert's general basis theorem for ideals), for invariants with restriction to integral coefficients, and finally she attacks the same question along with the question of a minimum basis consisting of independent elements for fields of rational functions.

Already in Erlangen about 1913 Emmy lectured occasionally, substituting for her father when he was taken ill. She must have been to Göttingen about that time, too, but I suppose only on a visit with her brother Fritz. At least I remember him much better than her from my time as a Göttinger *Privatdozent,* 1910–1913. During the war, in 1916, Emmy came to Göttingen for good; it was due to Hilbert's and Klein's direct influence that she stayed. Hilbert at that time was over head and ears in the general theory of relativity, and for Klein, too, the theory of relativity and its connection with his old ideas of the Erlangen program brought the last flareup of his mathematical interests and mathematical production. The second volume of his history of mathematics in the nineteenth century bears witness thereof. To both Hilbert and Klein Emmy was welcome as she was able to help them with her invariant theoretic knowledge. For two of the most significant sides of the general relativity theory she gave at that time the genuine and universal mathematical formulation: First, the reduction of the problem of differential invariants to a purely algebraic one by use of "normal coordinates"; second, the identities between the left sides of Euler's equations of a problem of variation which occur when the (multiple) integral is invariant with respect to a group of transformations involving arbitrary functions (identities that contain the conservation theorem of energy and momentum in the case of invariance with respect to arbitrary transformations of the four world coordinates).

Still during the war, Hilbert tried to push through Emmy Noether's *Habilitation* in the Philosophical Faculty in Göttingen. He failed due to the resistance of the philologists and historians. It is a well-known anecdote that Hilbert supported her application by declaring at the faculty meeting, "I do not see that the sex of the candidate is an argument against her admission as *Privatdozent*. After all, we are a university and not a bathing establishment." Probably he provoked the adversaries even more by that remark. Nevertheless, she was able to give lectures in Göttingen, that were announced under Hilbert's name. But in 1919, after the end of the War and the proclamation of the German Republic had changed the conditions, her *Habilitation* became possible. In 1922 there followed her nomination as a *nicht-beamteter ausserordentlicher Professor*; this was a mere title carrying no obligations and no salary. She was, however, entrusted with a *Lehrauftrag* for algebra, which carried a modest remuneration.

During the wild times after the Revolution of 1918, she did not keep aloof from the political excitement, she sided more or less with the Social Democrats; without being actually in party life she participated intensely in the discussion of the political and social problems of the day. One of her first pupils, Grete Hermann, belonged to Nelson's philosophic-political circle in Göttingen. It is hardly imaginable nowadays how willing the young generation in Germany was at that time for a fresh start, to try to build up Germany, Europe, society in general, on the foundations of reason, humaneness, and justice. But alas! the mood among the academic youth soon enough veered around; in the struggles that shook Germany during the following years and which took on the form of civil war here and there, we find them mostly on the side of the reactionary and nationalistic forces. Responsible for this above all was the breaking by the Allies of the promise of Wilson's Fourteen Points, and the fact that Republican Germany came to feel the victors' fist not less hard than the Imperial Reich could have; in particular, the youth were embittered by the national defamation added to the enforcement of a grim peace treaty. It was then that the great opportunity for the pacification of Europe was lost, and the seed sown for the disastrous development we are the witnesses of. In later years Emmy Noether took no part in matters political. She always remained, however, a convinced pacifist, a stand which she held very important and serious.

In the modest position of a *nichtbeamteter ausserordentlicher Professor* she worked in Göttingen until 1933, during the last years in the beautiful new Mathematical Institute that had risen in Göttingen chiefly by Courant's energy and the generous financial help of the Rockefeller Foundation. I have a vivid recollection of her when I was in Göttingen as visiting professor in the winter semester of 1926–1927, and lectured on representations of continuous groups. She was in the audience; for just at that time the hypercomplex number systems and their representations had caught her interest and I remember many discussions when I walked home after the lectures, with her and von Neumann, who was in Göttingen as a Rockefeller Fellow, through the cold, dirty, rain-wet streets of Göttingen. When I was called permanently to Göttingen in 1930, I earnestly tried to obtain from the Ministerium a better position for her, because I was ashamed to occupy such a preferred position beside her whom I knew to be my superior as a mathematician in many respects. I did not succeed, nor did an attempt to push through her election as a member of the Göttinger Gesellschaft der Wissenschaften. Tradition, prejudice, external considerations, weighted the balance against her scientific merits and scientific greatness, by that time denied by no one. In my Göttingen years, 1930–1933, she was without doubt the strongest center of mathematical activity there, considering both the fertility of her scientific research program and her influence upon a large circle of pupils.

Her development into that great independent master whom we admire today was relatively slow. Such a late maturing is a rare phenomenon in mathematics; in most cases the great creative impulses lie in early youth. Sophus Lie, like Emmy Noether, is one of the few great exceptions. Not until 1920, thirteen years after her promotion, appeared in the Mathematische Zeitschrift that paper of hers written with Schmeidler, "Über Moduln in nicht-kommutativen Bereichen, insbesondere aus Differential- und Differenzen-Ausdrücken", which seems to mark the decisive turning point. It is here for the first time that the Emmy Noether appears whom we all know, and who changed the face of algebra by her work. Above all, her conceptual axiomatic way of thinking in algebra becomes first noticeable in this paper dealing with differential operators as they are quite common nowadays in quantum mechanics. In performing them, one after the other, their composition, which may be interpreted as a kind of multiplication, is not commutative. But instead of operating with the formal expressions, the simple properties of the operations of addition and multiplication to which they lend themselves are formulated as axioms at the beginning of the investigation, and these axioms then form the basis of all further reasoning. A similar procedure has remained typical for Emmy Noether from then on. Later I shall try to characterize this world of algebra as a whole in which the scene of her mathematical activities was laid.

Not less characteristic for Emmy was her collaboration with another, in this case with Schmeidler. I suppose that Schmeidler gave as much as he received in this cooperation. In later years, however, Emmy Noether frequently acted as the true originator; she was most generous in sharing her ideas with others. She had many pupils, and one of the chief methods of her research was to expound her ideas in a still unfinished state in lectures, and then discuss them with her pupils. Sometimes she lectured on the same subject one semester after another, the whole subject taking on a better ordered and more unified shape every time, and gaining of course in the substance of results. It is obvious that this method sometimes put enormous demands upon her audience. In general, her lecturing was certainly not good in technical respects. For that she was too erratic and she cared too little for a nice and well arranged form. And yet she was an inspired teacher; he who was capable of adjusting himself entirely to her, could learn very much from her. Her significance for algebra cannot be read entirely from her own papers; she had great stimulating power and many of her suggestions took final shape only in the works of her pupils or co-workers. A large part of what is contained in the second volume of van der Waerden's *Modern Algebra* must be considered her property. The same is true of parts of Deuring's recently published book on algebras in which she collaborated intensively. Hasse acknowledges that he owed the suggestion for his beautiful papers on the connection between hypercomplex quantities and the theory of class fields to casual remarks by Emmy Noether. She could just utter a far-seeking remark like this, "Norm rest symbol is nothing else than cyclic algebra" in her prophetic lapidary manner, out of her mighty imagination that hit the mark most of the time and gained in strength in the course of years; and such a remark could then become a signpost to point the way for difficult future work. And one cannot read the scope of her accomplishments from the individual results of her papers alone: she originated above all a new and epoch-making style of thinking in algebra.

She lived in close communion with her pupils; she loved them, and took interest in their personal affairs. They formed a somewhat noisy and stormy family, "the Noether boys" as we called them in Göttingen.

Among her pupils proper I may name Grete Hermann, Krull, Hölzer, Grell, Koethe, Deuring, Fitting, Witt, Tsen, Shoda, Levitzki. F. K. Schmidt is strongly influenced by her, chiefly through Krull's mediation. V. d. Waerden came to her from Holland as a more or less finished mathematician and with ideas of his own; but he learned from Emmy Noether the apparatus of notions and the kind of thinking that permitted him to formulate his ideas and to solve his problems. Artin and Hasse stand beside her as two independent minds whose field of production touches on hers closely, though both have a stronger arithmetical texture. With Hasse above all she collaborated very closely during her last years. From different sides, Richard Brauer and she dealt with the profounder structural problems of algebras, she in a more abstract spirit, Brauer, educated in the school of the great algebraist I. Schur, more concretely operating with matrices and representations of groups; this, too, led to an extremely fertile cooperation. She held a rather close friendship with Alexandroff in Moscow, who came frequently as a guest to Göttingen. I believe that her mode of thinking has not been without influence upon Alexandroff's topological investigations. About 1930 she spent a semester in Moscow and there got into close touch with Pontrjagin also. Before that, in 1928–1929, she had lectured for one semester in

Frankfurt while Siegel delivered a course of lectures as a visitor in Göttingen.

In the spring of 1933 the storm of the National Revolution broke over Germany. The Göttinger Mathematisch-Naturwissenschaftliche Fakultät, for the building up and consolidation of which Klein and Hilbert had worked for decades, was struck at its roots. After an interregnum of one day by Neugebauer, I had to take over the direction of the Mathematical Institute. But Emmy Noether, as well as many others, was prohibited from participation in all academic activities, and finally her venia legendi, as well as her *Lehrauftrag* and the salary going with it, were withdrawn. A stormy time of struggle like this one we spent in Göttingen in the summer of 1933 draws people closer together; thus I have a particularly vivid recollection of these months. Emmy Noether, her courage, her frankness, her unconcern about her own fate, her conciliatory spirit, were in the midst of all the hatred and meanness, despair and sorrow surrounding us, a moral solace. It was attempted, of course, to influence the Ministerium and other responsible and irresponsible but powerful bodies so that her position might be saved. I suppose there could hardly have been in any other case such a pile of enthusiastic testimonials filed with the Minis-

terium as was sent in on her behalf. At that
time we really fought; there was still hope
left that the worst could be warded off. It was
in vain. Franck, Born, Courant, Landau,
Emmy Noether, Neugebauer, Bernays and
others—scholars the university had before
been proud of—had to go because the possibility of working was taken away from them.
Göttingen scattered into the four winds! This
fate brought Emmy Noether to Bryn Mawr,
and the short time she taught here and as
guest at our Institute for Advanced Study in
Princeton is still too fresh in our memory to
need to be spoken of. She harbored no
grudge against Göttingen and her fatherland
for what they had done to her. She broke no
friendship on account of political dissension.
Even last summer she returned to Göttingen,
and lived and worked there as though all
things were as before. She was sincerely glad
that Hasse was endeavoring with success to
rebuild the old, honorable and proud
mathematical tradition of Göttingen even in
the changed political circumstances. But she
had adjusted herself with perfect ease to her
new American surroundings, and her girl
students here were as near to her heart as the
Noether boys had been in Göttingen. She was
happy at Bryn Mawr; and indeed perhaps
never before in her life had she received so
many signs of respect, sympathy, friendship,

as were bestowed upon her during her last one and half years at Bryn Mawr. Now we stand at her grave.

It shall not be forgotten what America did during these last two stressful years for Emmy Noether and for German science in general.

If this sketch of her life is to be followed by a short synopsis of her work and her human and scientific personality, I must attempt to draw in a few strokes the scene of her work: the world of algebra. The system of real numbers, of so paramount import for the whole of mathematics and physics, resembles a Janus head with two faces: In one aspect it is the field of the algebraic operations + and ×, and their inversions. In the other aspect it is a continuous manifold, the parts of which are continuously connected with each other. The one is the algebraic, the other the topological face of numbers. Modern axiomatics, single-minded as it is and hence disliking this strange mixture of war and peace (in this respect differing from modern politics), carefully disjointed both parts.

Hence the pure algebraist can do nothing with his numbers except perform upon them the four species, addition, subtraction, multiplication, and division. For him, therefore, a set of numbers is closed, he has no means to get beyond it when these operations applied to any two numbers of the set always lead to

134

a number of the same set again. Such a set is called a domain of rationality or a field. The simplest field is the set of all rational numbers. Another example is the set of the numbers of the form $a + b \sqrt{2}$ where a and b are rational, the so-called algebraic number field ($\sqrt{2}$). The classical problem of algebra is the solution of an algebraic equation $f(x) = 0$ whose coefficients may lie in a field K, for instance the field of rational numbers. Knowing a root δ of the equation, one knows at the same time all numbers arising from δ (and the numbers of K) by means of the four species; they form the algebraic field $K(\delta)$ comprising K. Within this number field $K(\delta)$, δ itself plays the rôle of a determining number from which all other numbers can be rationally derived. But many, almost all, numbers of $K(\delta)$ can take the place of δ in this respect. It is, therefore, a great advance to replace the study of the equation $f(x) = 0$ by the study of the field $K(\delta)$. We thereby extinguish unessential features, we take uniformly into account all equations arising from the one $f(x) = 0$ by rational transformations of the unknown x, and we replace a formula, the equation $f(x) = 0$, which might seduce us to blind computations, by a notion, the notion of the field which one can get at only in a conceptual way.

Within the system of *integral* numbers the operations of addition, subtraction, and mul-

tiplication only allow unlimited perfor-
mance; division has to be canceled. Such a
domain is called a domain of integrity or a
ring. As the notion of integer is characteristic
of number theory, one may say: number
theory deals with rings instead of fields. The
polynomials of one variable or indeterminate
x are likewise such a domain of quantities as
we described to form a ring; the coefficients
of the polynomials might here be restricted to
a given number field or ring. Algebra does
not interpret the argument x to be a variable
varying over a continuous range of values; it
looks upon it as an indeterminate, an empty
symbol serving only to weld the coefficients
of the polynomial into a unified expression
which suggests in a natural way the rules of
addition and multiplication. The statement
that a polynomial vanishes means that all its
coefficients are zero rather than that the
function takes on the value zero for all values
of the independent variable. One is not for-
bidden to substitute an indeterminate x by a
number or by a polynomial of one or several
other indeterminates $y, z, \ldots$; however, this
is a formal process projecting the ring of
polynomials of x faithfully upon the ring of
numbers or of polynomials in $y, z, \ldots$.
Faithfully, that means preserving all rational
relations expressible in terms of the fundamental operations, addition, subtraction, multiplication.

Besides adjunction of indeterminates, algebra knows another procedure for forming new fields or rings. Let p be a prime number, for instance 5. We take the ordinary integers, agreeing, however, to consider numbers to be equal when they are congruent mod. p, i.e., when they give the same remainder under division by p. One may illustrate this by winding the line of numbers on a circle of circumference p. A peculiar field then arises consisting of p different elements only. To the *prime number* there corresponds within the ring of polynomials of a single variable x (with numerical coefficients taken from a given number field K) the *prime polynomial $p(x)$*. By considering two polynomials equal which are congruent modulo a given prime polynomial $p(x)$, the ring of all polynomials is changed into a *field* which possesses exactly the same algebraic properties as the number field $K(\delta)$ arising from the underlying number field K by adjoining a root δ of the equation $p(x) = 0$. But the present process goes on within pure algebra without requiring solution of an equation $p(x) = 0$ that is actually unsolvable in K. This interpretation of the algebraic number fields $K(\delta)$ was given by Kronecker after Cauchy had already founded the calculation with the imaginary number i on this idea.

In such a way one was led by degrees to erect algebra in a purely axiomatic manner.

A whole array of great mathematical names could be mentioned who initiated and developed this axiomatic trend: after Kronecker and Dedekind, E. H. Moore in America, Peano in Italy, Steinitz, and, above all, Hilbert in Germany. A field now is a realm of elements, called numbers, within which two operations + and × are defined, satisfying the usual axioms. If one leaves out the axiom of division which states the unique invertibility of multiplication, one gets a ring instead of a field. The fields no longer appear as parts cut out of that universal realm of numbers, the continuum of the real or complex numbers that the Calculus is concerned with, but every field is now, so to speak, a world in itself. One may join the elements of any field by operations, but not the elements of different fields. This standpoint that each object which is offered to mathematical analysis carries its own kind of numbers to be defined in terms of that object and its intrinsic constituents, instead of approaching every object by the same universal number system developed a priori and independently of the applications—this standpoint, I say, has gained ground more and more also in the axiomatic foundations of geometry and recently in a rather surprising manner in quantum physics. We are here confronted by one of those mysterious parallelisms in the development of mathematics and physics that might induce one to believe in a preestablished harmony between nature and mind.

When speaking of axiomatics, I was referring to the following methodical procedure: One separates in a natural way the different sides of a concretely given object of mathematical investigation, makes each of them accessible from its own relatively narrow and easily surveyable group of assumptions, and then by joining the partial results after appropriate specialization, returns to the complex whole. The last synthetic part is purely mechanical. The art lies in the first analytical part of breaking up the whole and generalizing the parts. One does not seek the general for the sake of generality, but the point is that each generalization simplifies by reducing the hypotheses and thus makes us understand certain sides of an unsurveyable whole. Whether a partition with corresponding generalization is natural, can hardly be judged by any other criterion than its fertility. If one systematizes this procedure which the individual investigator manages supported by all the analogies available to him by the mass of his mathematical experiences and with more or less inventive ability and sensitivity, one comes upon axiomatics. Hence axiomatics is today by no means merely a method for logical clarification and deepening of the foundations, but it has become a powerful weapon of concrete mathematical research itself. This method was applied by Emmy Noether with masterly skill, it suited her nature, and she made algebra the Eldorado of axiomatics. An important point is the ascertainment of the "right" general notions like field, ring, ideal, etc., the splitting-up of a proposition into partial propositions and their right generalizations by means of those general notions. This partition of the whole and screening off of the unessential features once accomplished, the proof of the individual steps does not cause any serious trouble in many cases. In a conference on topology and abstract algebra as two ways of mathematical understanding, in 1931, I said this:

> Nevertheless I should not pass over in silence the fact that today the feeling among mathematicians is beginning to spread that the fertility of these abstracting methods is approaching exhaustion. The case is this: that all these nice general notions do not fall into our laps by themselves. But definite concrete problems were first conquered in their undivided complexity, single-handed by brute force, so to speak. Only afterwards the axiomaticians came along and stated: Instead of breaking in the door with all your might and bruising your hands, you should have constructed such and such a key of skill, and by it you would have been able to open the door quite smoothly. But they can construct the key only because they

are able, after the breaking in was successful, to study the lock from within and without.
Before you can generalize, formalize and
axiomatize, there must be a mathematical substance. I think that the mathematical substance
in the formalizing of which we have trained
ourselves during the last decades, becomes
gradually exhausted. And so I foresee that the
generation now rising will have a hard time in
mathematics.

Emmy Noether protested against that: and
indeed she could point to the fact that just
during the last years the axiomatic method
had disclosed in her hands new, concrete,
profound problems by the application of
non-commutative algebra upon commutative fields and their number theory, and had
shown the way to their solution.

Emmy Noether's scientific production
seems to me to fall into three clearly distinct
epochs: (1) the period of relative dependence, 1907–1919; (2) the investigations
grouped around the general theory of ideals,
1920–26; (3) the study of the non-
commutative algebras, their representations
by linear transformations, and their application to the study of commutative number
fields and their arithmetics, from 1927 on.
The first epoch was described in the sketch of
her life. I should now like to say a few words
about the second epoch, the epoch of the
general theory of ideals.

The ideals had been devised by Dedekind in order to reestablish, by introducing appropriate ideal elements, the main law of unique decomposition of a number into prime factors that broke down in algebraic number fields. The thought consisted in replacing a number, like 6 for instance, in its property as a divisor by the set of all numbers divisible by 6; this set is called the ideal (6). In the same manner one may interpret the greatest common divisor of two numbers, a, b, as the set of all numbers of form $ax + by$ where x, y range independently over all integers. In the ring of ordinary integers this system is identical with a system of the multiples of a single number d, the greatest common divisor. This, however, is not the case in algebraic number fields, and hence it becomes necessary to admit as divisors not only numbers but also ideals. An ideal in a ring R then has to be defined as a subset of R such that sum and difference of two numbers of the ideal belong to the ideal as well as the product of a number of the ideal by an arbitrary number of the ring. Still, from another side, this notion appeared in algebraic geometry. An algebraic surface in space is defined by one algebraic equation $f = 0$; here f is a polynomial with respect to the coordinates. If one is to consider algebraic manifolds of fewer dimensions, one has to put down instead a finite system of algebraic equations $f_1 = 0$,

$f_2 = 0, \ldots, f_h = 0$. But then all polynomials
vanish upon the algebraic manifold which
arise by linear combination of the basic
polynomials $f_1, f_2, \ldots, f_h$ in the form $A_1 f_1 +$
$A_2 f_2 + \ldots + A_h f_h$ where the A's are quite
arbitrary polynomials. All the polynomials of
this kind form an ideal in the ring of polynomials; the algebraic manifold consists of the
points in which all polynomials of the ideal
vanish. With such ideals Hilbert's basis
theorem was concerned, one of the chief
tools in Hilbert's study of invariants; it asserts
that every ideal of polynomials has a finite
basis. Noether's residual theorem contains a
criterion that allows us to decide whether a
polynomial belongs to an ideal the members
of which have in common only a finite
number of zeros. For ideals of polynomials
Lasker—better known to nonmathematicians
as world chess champion for many years—
obtained results which showed that their
laws depart considerably from those met by
Dedekind in the algebraic number fields.

Consider, for instance, the following three
rings: the ring of ordinary integers, the rings
of polynomials of one and of two independent variables with rational coefficients. The
theorem of unique decomposition into prime
factors holds in each of them; but Euclid's
algorithm or the fact that the greatest common divisor of two elements, a, b, is contained in the ideal (a, b), i.e., can be ex-

pressed in the form $af + bg$ by means of two appropriate elements, f, g, of the ring, is true only in the first two cases. Indeed, in the domain of polynomials of two indeterminates x and y, the polynomials x and y themselves have no common divisor; nevertheless an equation like $1 = xf + yg$ where f and g are two polynomials, is impossible as the right side vanishes at the origin $x = 0$, $y = 0$.

Emmy Noether developed a general theory of ideals on an axiomatic basis that comprised all cases. Her chief axiom is the Teilerkettensatz: the hypothesis that a chain of ideals a_1, a_2, a_3, . . . necessarily comes to an end after a finite number of steps if each term a_i comprises the preceding a_{i-1} as a proper part. By her abstract theory many important developments of mathematics are welded together. Moreover, she showed how one can descend in the same axiomatic manner to the polynomial ideals on the one hand, and to the classical case of ideals in algebraic number fields on the other hand. In some instances her general theory passes even beyond what was known before through Lasker for polynomial ideals.

Until now we have stuck to all axioms satisfied by the ordinary numbers. There exist, however, strong motives for abandoning the commutative law of multiplication. Indeed, operations like the rotations of a rigid body in space, are entities which behave with respect to their composition in a non-commutative fashion: for the composition of two rotations it really matters whether one first performs the first and then the second, or does it in inverse order. Composition is here considered as a kind of multiplication. Rotations when expressed in terms of coordinates are linear transformations. The linear transformations, as they are capable of addition and composition or multiplication, form the most important example of non-commutative quantities. One therefore attempts to realize any given abstract non-commutative ring or "algebra" of quantities by linear transformations without destroying the relations established among them by the fundamental operations $+$ and $\times$; this is the aim of the theory of representations. The theory of non-commutative algebras and their representations was built up by Emmy Noether in a new unified, purely conceptual manner by making use of all results that had been accumulated by the ingenious labors of decades through Molien, Frobenius, Dickson, Wedderburn, and others. The notion of the ideal in several new versions again plays the decisive part. Besides it, the idea of *automorphism* proves to be rather useful, i.e., of those mappings one can perform within an algebra without destroying the internal relations. Calculative tools are discarded like, for instance, a certain determinant the nonvanishing of which Dedekind had used as a criterion for semi-simplicity; this was the more desirable as this criterion fails in some domains of rationality. In intense coopera-tion with Hasse and with Brauer she investi-. gated the structure of non-commutative algebras and applied the theory by means of her *verschränktes Produkt* (cross product) to the ordinary commutative number fields and their arithmetics. The most important papers of this epoch are "Hyperkomplexe Grössen und Darstellungstheorie", 1929; "Nicht-kommutative Algebra", 1933; and three smaller papers about norm rests and the prin-cipal genus theorem. Her theory of cross products was published by Hasse in connec-tion with his investigations about the theory of cyclic algebras. A common paper by Brauer, Hasse, and Emmy Noether proving the fact that every simple algebra over an or-dinary algebraic number field is cyclic in Dickson's sense, will remain a high mark in the history of algebra.

I must forego giving a picture of the con-tent of these profound investigations. In-stead, I had better try to close with a short general estimate of Emmy Noether as a mathematician and as a personality.

Her strength lay in her ability to operate abstractly with concepts. It was not necessary for her to allow herself to be led to new re-sults on the leading strings of known concrete examples. This had the disadvantage, however, that she was sometimes but incompletely cognizant of the specific details of the more interesting applications of her general theories. She possessed a most vivid imagination, with the aid of which she could visualize remote connections; she constantly strove toward unification. In this she sought out the essentials in the known facts, brought them into order by means of appropriate general concepts, espied the vantage point from which the whole could best be surveyed, cleansed the object under consideration of superfluous dross, and thereby won through to so simple and distinct a form that the venture into new territory could be undertaken with the greatest prospect of success. This clarifying power she proved, for example, in her theory of the cross product, in which almost all the facts had already been found by Dickson and by Brauer. She possessed a strong drive toward axiomatic purity. All should be accomplished within the frame and with the aid of the intrinsic properties of the structure under investigation; nothing should be brought from without, and only invariant processes should be applied. Thus it seemed to her that the use of matrices which commute with all the elements of a given matric algebra, so often to be found in the work of Schur, was inappropriate; accordingly she used the automorphisms instead. This can be carried too far, however, as when she disdained to employ a primitive element in the development of the Galois theory. She once said:

> If one proves the equality of two numbers a and b by showing first that $a \leq b$ and then $a \geq b$, it is unfair; one should instead show that they are really equal by disclosing the inner ground for their equality.

Of her predecessors in algebra and number theory, Dedekind was most closely related to her. For him she felt a deep veneration. She expected her students to read Dedekind's appendices to Dirichlet's "Zahlentheorie" not only in one, but in all editions. She took a most active part in the editing of Dedekind's works; here the attempt was made to indicate, after each of Dedekind's papers, the modern development built upon his investigations. Her affinity with Dedekind, who was perhaps the most typical Lower Saxon among German mathematicians, proves by a glaring example how illusory it is to associate in a schematic way race with the style of mathematical thought. In addition to Dedekind's work, that of Steinitz on the theory of abstract fields was naturally of great importance for her own work. She lived through a great flowering of algebra in Germany, toward which she contributed much. Her methods need not, however, be considered the only means of salvation. In addition to Artin and Hasse, who in some respects are akin to her, there are algebraists of a still more different stamp, such as I. Schur in Germany, Dickson and Wedderburn in America, whose achievements are certainly not behind hers in depth and significance. Perhaps her followers, in pardonable enthusiasm, have not always fully recognized this fact.

Emmy Noether was a zealous collaborator in the editing of the *Mathematische Annalen.* That this work was never explicitly recognized may have caused her some pain.

It was only too easy for those who met her for the first time, or had no feeling for her creative power, to consider her queer and to make fun at her expense. She was heavy of build and loud of voice, and it was often not easy for one to get the floor in competition with her. She preached mightily, and not as the scribes. She was a rough and simple soul, but her heart was in the right place. Her frankness was never offensive in the least degree. In everyday life she was most unassuming and utterly unselfish; she had a kind and friendly nature. Nevertheless she enjoyed the recognition paid her; she could answer with a bashful smile like a young girl to whom one had whispered a compliment. No one could contend that the Graces had stood by her cradle; but if we in Göttingen often chaffingly referred to her as "der Noether" (with the masculine article), it was also done with a respectful recognition of her power as a creative thinker who seemed to have broken through the barrier of sex. She possessed a rare humor and a sense of sociability; a tea in her apartments could be most pleasurable. But she was a one-sided being who was thrown out of balance by the overweight of her mathematical talent. Essential aspects of human life remained undeveloped in her, among them, I suppose, the erotic, which, if we are to believe the poets, is for many of us the strongest source of emotions, raptures, desires, and sorrows, and conflicts. Thus she sometimes gave the impression of an unwieldy child, but she was a kind-hearted and courageous being, ready to help, and capable of the deepest loyalty and affection. And of all I have known, she was certainly one of the happiest.

Comparison with the other woman mathematician of world renown, Sonya Kovalevskaya, suggests itself. Sonya had certainly the more complete personality, but was also of a much less happy nature. In order to pursue her studies Sonya had to defy the opposition of her parents, and entered into a marriage in name only, although it did not quite remain so. Emmy Noether had, as I have already indicated, neither a rebellious nature nor Bohemian leanings. Sonya possessed feminine charm, instincts, and vanity; social successes were by no means immaterial to her. She was a creature of tension and whims; mathematics made her unhappy, whereas Emmy found the greatest pleasure in her work. Sonya followed literary pursuits outside of mathematics. In her later years in Paris, as she worked feverishly on a paper to be submitted for a mathematical prize, Sonya, alluding in a letter to a certain M. with whom she was in love, wrote "The fat M. occupies all the room on my couch and in my thoughts." Such was Sonya: you see the tension between her creative mind and life with its passion and the self-mocking spirit ironically viewing her own desperate conflict. How far from Emmy's possibilities! But Emmy Noether without doubt possessed by far the greater power, the greater scientific talent.

Indeed, two traits determined above all her nature: First, the native productive power of her mathematical genius. She was not clay, pressed by the artistic hands of God into a harmonious form, but rather a chunk of human primary rock into which he had blown his creative breath of life. Second, her heart knew no malice; she did not believe in evil—indeed it never entered her mind that it could play a role among men. This was never more forcefully apparent to me than in the last stormy summer, that of 1933, which we spent together in Göttingen. The memory of her work in science and of her personality among her fellows will not soon pass away. She was a great mathematician, the greatest, I firmly believe, that her sex has ever produced, and a great woman.

THE INSTITUTE FOR ADVANCED STUDY
PRINCETON, N.J.

In Memory of Emmy Noether

On September 5, 1935, the Moscow Mathematical Society held a commemorative meeting to honor the memory of Emmy Noether, who had died on April 14, 1935. In addition to members of the Society, the participants in the meeting included the brother of the deceased, Professor Fritz Noether of Tomsk University, and also mathematicians attending the First International Conference on Topology, which was taking place in Moscow at the same time. After a moment of silence was held in honor of the deceased, the Society's president, P. S. Aleksandrov, gave a eulogy, which is printed below. Then specialists presented reports on research connected with the works and mathematical ideas of Emmy Noether: J. von Neumann (Princeton, U.S.A.), A. Weil (Paris), and A. G. Kurosh (Moscow). These papers are published in the journal *Matematicheskii Sbornik*. At the conclusion of the meeting, Academician S. Lefschetz (Princeton, U.S.A.) gave a short speech in honor of the deceased. In his speech Prof. Lefschetz emphasized, in particular, the great value that Emmy Noether's ideas had for the development of modern topology.

In Memory of Emmy Noether

ADDRESS DELIVERED BY THE PRESIDENT OF THE MOSCOW
MATHEMATICAL SOCIETY, P. S. ALEXANDROV,
ON SEPTEMBER 5, 1935*

On April 14 of this year, in the small town of Bryn Mawr (Pennsylvania, U.S.A.), Emmy Noether, former professor at Göttingen Uni-

* Published in *Proceedings of the Moscow Mathematical Society*, 1936, 2.

versity and one of the foremost mathematicians of modern times, died at the age of 53 following an operation.

The death of Emmy Noether is not only a great loss for mathematical science, it is a tragedy in the full sense of the word. The greatest woman mathematician who ever lived died at the very height of her creative powers; she died, driven from her homeland and torn from the scientific school which she had created over the years and which had become one of the most brilliant schools of mathematics in Europe; she died, torn from her family, which had been scattered to different countries because of the same political barbarism that caused Emmy Noether herself to emigrate from Germany.

We of the Moscow Mathematical Society pay our respects today to the memory of one of our leading members, who for more than ten years maintained continual and close ties, constant scientific interaction, and sincere good will and friendship with the Society, with the Moscow mathematical community, with the mathematicians of the Soviet Union . . . Permit me in the name of the Society to express our deepest condolences to the brother of the deceased, Professor Fritz Noether, formerly of the Technische Hochschule in Breslau and currently of the Tomsk Mathematical Institute, who is with us today.

The biography of Emmy Noether is simple.
She was born on March 23, 1882 in Erlangen
to the family of the famous mathematician
Max Noether. Her mathematical talent developed slowly. A student of Gordan in Erlangen, she defended her dissertation in
1907; her work was on Gordan's formal
computational invariant theory. She often al-
luded to this dissertation afterwards, and always referred to it with disdainful epithets,
such as "Formelngestrüpp" [jungle of for-
malism (?)] and "Rechncrei" [routine computations (?)]. Despite all of this it should be
noted that Emmy Noether, the ardent foe of
computation and algorithms in mathematics,
herself was fully capable of mastering such
methods—this is proved not only by her first
dissertation, which in actual fact was not a
major work, but also by her subsequent papers on differential invariants (1918), which
have become classics. But in these papers we
already see the fundamental characteristic of
her mathematical talent: the striving for general formulations of mathematical problems
and the ability to find the formulation which
reveals the essential logical nature of the
question, stripped of any incidental pecu-
liarities which complicate matters and obscure
the fundamental point.

She wrote the papers on differential invariants when she was still in Göttingen, where
she had moved in 1916. Her work of this

period was heavily influenced by Hilbert. It is often forgotten that in this period Emmy Noether obtained excellent results concerning the concrete algebraic problems of Hilbert. These results and her work on differential invariants would have been enough by themselves to earn her the reputation of a first class mathematician and are hardly less of a contribution to mathematics than the famous research of S. V. Kovalevskaya. But when we think of Emmy Noether as a mathematician, we have in mind not these early works, important though they were in their concrete results, but rather the main period of her research, beginning in about 1920, when she became the creator of a new direction in algebra and the leading, the most consistent and prominent representative of a certain general mathematical doctrine—all that which is characterized by the words "begriffliche Mathematik" [abstract mathematics].

Emmy Noether herself is partly responsible for the fact that her work of the early period is rarely given the attention that it would naturally deserve. With the singlemindedness that was part of her nature, she herself was ready to forget what she had done in the early years of her scientific life, since she considered those results to have been a diversion from the main path of her research, which was the creation of a general, abstract algebra.

It is not my task to analyze and illuminate everything that Emmy Noether did in mathematics. In the first place, not being an algebraist, I do not consider myself qualified to perform such a task. In the second place, to the extent appropriate for an obituary, this task was performed in an excellent and completely competent manner by Hermann Weyl (in an address delivered at a commemorative meeting in honor of Emmy Noether on April 26, 1935 at Bryn Mawr, Pennsylvania, U.S.A., and published in *Scripta Mathematica*, v. III, no. 3, June 1935) and by van der Waerden (*Mathematische Annalen*, v. 111, 1935, p. 469). My purpose today is somewhat different: I would like to evoke for you as accurate an image as possible of the deceased, as a mathematician, as the head of a large scientific school, as a brilliant, original, and fascinating personality.

Emmy Noether embarked on her own completely original mathematical path in the years 1919/1920. She herself dated the beginning of this fundamental period in her work with the famous joint work with W. Schmeidler (*Mathematische Zeitschrift*, v. 8, 1920). In a sense this paper serves as a prologue to her general theory of ideals, which she revealed in 1921 in the classic memoir

"Idealtheorie in Ringbereichen." I believe that, of everything that Emmy Noether did, it is the foundations of general ideal theory and everything connected with this that has had, is continuing to have, and will have in the future the greatest impact on mathematics as a whole. Not only have these ideas already led to many specific fundamental applications—for example, in van der Waerden's work on algebraic geometry—moreover, they have had an essential influence on algebraic thinking itself, and in certain respects on general mathematical thinking, in our times. If the development of mathematics today is moving forward under the sign of algebraization, the penetration of algebraic ideas and methods into the most diverse mathematical theories, then this only became possible after the work of Emmy Noether. It was she who taught us to think in terms of simple and general algebraic concepts—homeomorphic mappings, groups and rings with operators, ideals—and not in terms of cumbersome algebraic computations; and thereby opened up the path to finding algebraic principles in places where such principles had been obscured by some complicated special situation which was not at all suited for the accustomed approach of the classical algebraists. Theorems such as the "homeomorphism and isomorphism theorem", concepts such as the ascending

and descending chain conditions for sub-
groups and ideals, or the notion of groups
with operators, were first introduced by
Emmy Noether and have entered into the
daily practice of a wide range of mathematical disciplines as a powerful and constantly
applicable tool, even though these disciplines
may concern subjects which have no relation
to the work of Emmy Noether herself. We
need only glance at Pontryagin's work on the
theory of continuous groups, the recent work
of Kolmogorov on the combinatorial topology of locally bicompact spaces, the work of
Hopf on the theory of continuous mappings,
to say nothing of van der Waerden's work on
algebraic geometry, in order to sense the influence of Emmy Noether's ideas. This influence is also keenly felt in H. Weyl's book
Gruppentheorie und Quantenmechanik.

I have purposely indicated areas of mathematics which are different from the direct
subject of Emmy Noether's research; if one
speaks of algebra itself (including group
theory), then we see that she created a major
new direction in which a large number of
very talented mathematicians work, continuing the research of Emmy Noether in many
concrete areas. In particular, general elimination theory and the theory of algebraic var-
ieties are among the most significant
achievements that have arisen on the
groundwork of Emmy Noether's general

ideal theory. In connection with what I have just said, I would like to recall that, among the major works of algebra that we have produced here in Moscow over the last decade, the famous work of O. Yu. Schmidt on unique direct product decomposition of groups, and also the work of A. G. Kurosh, were heavily influenced by Emmy Noether.

Despite all of the concrete and constructive explicit results of Emmy Noether that came out of the various creative periods in her life, there can be no doubt that the fundamental strength and the fundamental dynamism of her talent went in the direction of general mathematical conceptions having a marked axiomatic coloration. The present moment is especially opportune for subjecting this side of her creativity to detailed analysis—not only because the question of the general and the special, the abstract and the concrete, the axiomatic and the constructive is now one of the sharpest questions in our mathematical life. Interest in this entire problem is especially pertinent because, on the one hand, the mathematical journals have undoubtedly become over-burdened with a great number of articles which generalize, axiomatize and so on, often without any concrete mathematical content; on the other hand, from time to time one hears proclamations to the effect that the only true mathematics is that which is "classical." This slogan sweeps aside impor-

tant mathematical problems only because
they contradict one or another habit of
thought, because they make use of concepts
which were not in use a few decades ago,
such as, for example, the concepts of general
algebraic rings and fields, of topological and
function spaces, and many others. In the
obituary cited above, H. Weyl also poses this
question. His words on this subject so pene-
trate to the heart of the matter that I cannot
refrain from citing them in their entirety:

In a conference on topology and abstract
algebra as two ways of mathematical understanding, in 1931, I said this:
Nevertheless I should not pass over in silence the fact that today the feeling among
mathematicians is beginning to spread that
the fertility of these abstracting methods is
approaching exhaustion. The case is this:
that all these nice general notions do not fall
into our laps by themselves. But definite
concrete problems were first conquered in
their undivided complexity, singlehanded by
brute force, so to speak. Only afterwards the
axiomaticians came along and stated: Instead of breaking in the door with all your
might and bruising your hands, you should
have constructed such and such a key of
skill, and by it you would have been able to
open the door quite smoothly. But they can
construct the key only because they are able,
after the breaking in was successful, to study
the lock from within and without. Before

you can generalize, formalize and
axiomatize, there must be a mathematical
substance. I think that the mathematical
substance in the formalizing of which we
have trained ourselves during the last decades, becomes gradually exhausted. And so
I foresee that the generation now rising will
have a hard time in mathematics.

"Emmy Noether," continues Weyl, "protested against that: and indeed she could
point to the fact that just during the last years
the axiomatic method had disclosed in her
hands new, concrete, profound problems . . . and had shown the way to their
solution."
Much in this quotation deserves our attention. In the first place, one cannot, of course,
dispute the point of view that every axiomatic presentation of a mathematical theory
must be preceded by a concrete, one might
say a naive mastery of it; that, moreover,
axiomatics is only interesting when it relates
to tangible mathematical knowledge (what
Weyl calls "mathematical substance"), and is
not tilting at windmills, so to speak. All of this
is indisputable, and, of course, it was not
against this that Emmy Noether protested.
What she protested against was the pes-
simism that shows through the last words of
the quotation from Weyl's speech of 1931;
the substance of human knowledge, includ-

ing mathematical knowledge, is inexhaustible, at least for the foreseeable future—this is what Emmy Noether firmly believed. The "substance *of the last decades*" may be exhausted, but not mathematical substance in general which is connected by thousands of intricate threads with the reality of the external world and human existence. Emmy Noether deeply felt this connection between all great mathematics, even the most abstract, and the real world; even if she did not think this through philosophically, she intuited it with all of her being as a great scientist and as a lively person who was not at all imprisoned in abstract schemes. For Emmy Noether mathematics was always knowledge of reality, and not a game of symbols; she protested fervently whenever the representatives of those areas of mathematics which are directly connected with applications wanted to appropriate for themselves the claim to tangible knowledge. In mathematics, as in knowledge of the world, both aspects are equally valuable: the accumulation of facts and concrete constructions and the establishment of general principles which overcome the isolation of each fact and bring the factual knowledge to a new stage of axiomatic understanding.

A profound feeling for reality lay at the foundation of Emmy Noether's mathematical creativity; her entire scientific personality opposed the tendency (which is widespread in many mathematical circles) to transform mathematics into a game, into some sort of peculiar mental sport. In the numerous conversations I had with her about the nature of mathematical knowledge and creativity, most of which were naive discussions in the sense that we did not enter into a truly philosophical statement of the question, I often—with her evident sympathy—recalled my favorite quotation from Laplace: "Si l'homme s'était borné à recueillir des faits, la science ne serait qu'une nomenclature stérile et jamais il n'eut connu les grandes lois de la nature." [If man had limited himself to the accumulation of facts, then science would have been merely a fruitless nomenclature, and he would never have learned the great laws of nature.] These words, spoken by one of the most prominent representatives of physical knowledge, by a scientist who had both feet firmly on the ground, contain an entire program of interrelations between the concrete and the abstract in human thought in general, and in mathematics in particular. And it seems to me that Emmy Noether brought this program to realization in her work.

In 1924–1925 Emmy Noether's school made one of its most brilliant discoveries: the student van der Waerden from Amsterdam. He was then 22 years old, and was one of the brightest young mathematical talents of

Europe. Van der Waerden quickly mastered Emmy Noether's theories, added significant new results, and, more than anyone else, helped to make her ideas widely known. The course on general ideal theory which van der Waerden gave in Göttingen in 1927 was tremendously successful. In van der Waerden's brilliant presentation, the ideas of Emmy Noether overwhelmed the mathematical public, first in Göttingen and then in the other major mathematical centers of Europe. It is not surprising that Emmy Noether needed a popularizer for her ideas: her lectures were aimed at a small circle of students working in the area of her research and listening to her constantly. They were not at all suitable for a broad mathematical audience. To an outsider Emmy Noether seemed to lecture poorly, in a rapid and confusing manner; but her lectures contained a tremendous force of mathematical thought and an extraordinary warmth and enthusiasm. The same is true of her reports at meetings and congresses. Her lectures conveyed very much to a mathematician who already understood her ideas and was interested in her work; but a mathematician who was far from her research normally would have great difficulty understanding her exposition.

From 1927 on, as the influence of Emmy Noether's ideas on modern mathematics constantly increased, the scholarly renown of the author of those ideas was similarly increasing. Meanwhile, the direction of her own work was changing, moving more and more toward the areas of noncommutative algebra, representation theory and the general arithmetic of hypercomplex systems. The two most fundamental works of her later period show this trend: "Hyperkomplexe Grössen und Darstellungstheorie" (1929) and "Nichtkommutative Algebra" (1933), both published in *Mathematische Zeitschrift* (vol. 30 and 37). These and related papers immediately produced numerous reverberations in the work of algebraic number theorists, especially Hasse. Her best known student of this period was M. Deuring, who published a book "Algebren" in *Ergebnisse der Mathematik*, where he gave a survey of Emmy Noether's work on hypercomplex systems. In addition, her school included many young mathematicians who were starting their careers, such as Witt, Fitting, and others.

Emmy Noether lived to see the full recognition of her ideas. If in 1923–1925 she was striving to prove the importance of the theories she was developing, in 1932, at the International Congress of Mathematicians in Zurich, her accomplishments were lauded on all sides. The major survey talk that she gave at the Congress was a true triumph for the direction of research she represented. At that point she could look back upon the mathematical path she had traveled not only with an inner satisfaction, but with an awareness of her complete and unconditional recognition in the mathematical community. The Congress in Zurich marked the high point of her international scientific position. A few months later, German culture and, in particular, Göttingen University, which had nurtured that culture for centuries, were struck by the catastrophe of the fascist takeover, which in a matter of weeks scattered to the winds everything that had been painstakingly created over the years. What occurred was one of the greatest tragedies that had befallen human culture since the time of the Renaissance, a tragedy which only a few years ago had seemed impossible in twentieth-century Europe. One of its many victims was Emmy Noether's Göttingen school of algebraists. The leader of the school was driven from the halls of the university; having lost the right to teach, Emmy Noether was forced to emigrate from Germany. She accepted an invitation from the women's college in Bryn Mawr (1933), where she lived for the last year and a half of her life.

EMMY NOETHER'S career was full of paradoxes, and will always stand as an example of shocking stagnancy and inability to overcome prejudice on the part of the

Prussian academic and civil service bureaucracies. Her appointment as *Privatdozent* in 1919 was only possible because of the persistence of Hilbert and Klein, who overcame some extreme opposition from reactionary university circles. The basic formal objection was the sex of the candidate: "How can we allow a woman to become a *Privatdozent:* after all, once she is a *Privatdozent*, she may become a Professor and member of the University Senate; is it permissible for a woman to enter the Senate?" This provoked Hilbert's famous reply: "Meine Herren, der Senat ist ja keine Badenanstalt, warum darf eine Frau nicht dorthin!" [Gentlemen, the Senate is not a bathhouse, so I do not see why a woman cannot enter it!] In actual fact, the opposition of influential representatives of reactionary academic circles was caused not only and not even primarily because Emmy Noether was a woman, but by her well-known and very radical political beliefs, along with the aggravating circumstance in their eyes of her Jewish nationality. But I shall return to this later.

Eventually she received the appointment as *Privatdozent*, and later as honorary Professor; as a result of Courant's efforts she received a so-called *Lehrauftrag*, i.e., a small salary (200–400 marks per month) for her lectures, which required reconfirmation every year by the Ministry. It was in this position, without even a guaranteed salary, that she lived until the moment she was dismissed from the university and forced to leave Germany. She was not a member of a single academy, including the academy of the city whose university was the setting for all of her research. Here is what H. Weyl writes about this in his obituary:

> When I was called permanently to Göttingen in 1930,[1] I earnestly tried to obtain from the Ministerium a better position for her, because I was ashamed to occupy such a preferred position beside her whom I knew to be my superior as a mathematician in many respects. I did not succeed, nor did an attempt to push through her election as a member of the Göttinger Gesellschaft der Wissenschaften.[2] Tradition, prejudice, external considerations, weighted the balance against her scientific merits and scientific greatness, by that time denied by no one. In my Göttingen years, 1930–1933, she was without doubt the strongest center of mathematical activity there,

[1] In 1930 Hermann Weyl received Hilbert's chair at Göttingen, after Hilbert reached the maximum age (68) for occupying the position. Hilbert's chair was considered the foremost chair of mathematics in Germany, and carried with it a higher salary. After Weyl emigrated to America in 1933, Hasse occupied the position.

[2] The Göttingen academy of sciences, which was founded in 1742 in the Hanover period, was, following the model of the British academies of science, called the Royal Society of Science—Königliche Gesellschaft der Wissenschaften zu Göttingen.

considering both the fertility of her scientific research program and her influence upon a large circle of pupils."

It would be hard for me to add anything to these words of Weyl.

EMMY NOETHER had close ties to Moscow. Her connection with Moscow began in 1923, when Pavel Samuilovich Uryson, who has now also passed away, and I first went to Göttingen and immediately found ourselves in the mathematical circle led by Emmy Noether. The basic features of the Noether school struck us right away: the intellectual enthusiasm of its leader, which was transmitted to all of her students, her deep conviction in the importance and mathematical fertility of her ideas (a conviction which far from everyone shared at that time, even in Göttingen), and the extraordinary simplicity and warmth of the relations between the head of the school and her pupils. At that time the school consisted almost entirely of young Göttingen students; the period when it became international in its composition and was recognized as the most important center of algebraic thought in terms of its international impact, was still in the future.

The mathematical interests of Emmy Noether (who was then at the height of her work on general ideal theory) and the mathematical interests of Uryson and myself, which were then centered around problems in so-called abstract topology, had many points of contact with one another, and soon brought us together in constant, almost daily mathematical discussions. Emmy Noether was not, however, only interested in our topological work; she was interested in everything mathematical (and not only mathematical!) that was being done in Soviet Russia. She did not hide her sympathy toward our country and its social and governmental structure, despite the fact that such expressions of sympathy were considered shocking and improper by most representatives of Western European academic circles. It went so far that Emmy Noether was literally expelled from one of the Göttingen boarding-houses (where she lived and dined) at the insistence of the student boarders, who did not want to live under the same roof as a "pro-Marxist Jew"—an excellent prologue to the drama that came at the end of her life in Germany.

And Emmy Noether was sincerely glad of the scientific and mathematical successes of the Soviet Union, since she saw in this a decisive refutation of all of the prattle about how "the Bolsheviks are destroying culture," and she felt the approaching blossoming of a great new culture. Though the representative of one of the most abstract areas of mathematics, she distinguished herself with an amazing sensitivity in understanding the great historic transformations of our times; she always had a lively interest in politics, with all of her being she hated war and chauvinism in all of its manifestations, in this area she never wavered. Her sympathies were always steadfastly with the Soviet Union, where she saw the beginning of a new era in the history of mankind and a firm support for everything progressive in human thought. This feature was such a shining aspect of Emmy Noether's character, it left such a deep imprint on her entire personality, that to be silent about it would signify a tendentious distortion of Emmy Noether's nature as a scientist and as a person.

The scientific and personal friendship between Emmy Noether and me which started in 1923, continued until her death. Referring to this friendship, Weyl says in his obituary: "She held a rather close friendship with Alexandrov in Moscow. I believe that her mode of thinking has not been without influence upon Alexandrov's topological investigations." I am happy to take this opportunity to confirm the accuracy of Weyl's supposition. Emmy Noether's influence on my own and on other topological research in Moscow was very great and affected the very essence of our work. In particular, my theory of continuous partitions of topological spaces arose to a large extent under the influence of conversations with her in December to January of 1925–1926, when we were both in Holland. On the other hand, this was also the time when Emmy Noether's first ideas on the set theoretic foundations of group theory arose, serving as the subject for her course of lectures in the summer of 1926. In their original form these ideas were not developed further, but later she returned to them several times. The reason for this delay is probably the difficulty involved in axiomatizing the notion of a group starting from its partition into cosets as the fundamental concept. But the *idea* of a set-theoretic analysis of the concept of a group itself turned out to be fruitful, as shown by the recent work of Ore, Kurosh, and others.

Subsequent years saw a strengthening and deepening of Emmy Noether's topological interests. In the summers of 1926 and 1927 she went to the courses on topology which Hopf and I gave at Göttingen. She rapidly became oriented in a field that was completely new for her, and she continually made observations, which were often deep and subtle. When in the course of our lectures she first became acquainted with a systematic construction of combinatorial topology, she immediately observed that it would be worthwhile to study directly the groups of algebraic complexes and cycles of a given polyhedron and the subgroup of the cycle group consisting of cycles homologous to zero; instead of the usual definition of Betti numbers and torsion coefficients, she suggested immediately defining the Betti *group* as the complementary (quotient) group of the group of all cycles by the subgroup of cycles homologous to zero. This observation now seems self-evident. But in those years (1925–1928) this was a completely new point of view, which did not immediately encounter a sympathetic response on the part of many very authoritative topologists. Hopf and I immediately adopted Emmy Noether's point of view in this matter, but for some time we were among a small number of mathematicians who shared this viewpoint. These days it would never occur to anyone to construct combinatorial topology in any way other than through the theory of abelian groups; it is thus all the more fitting to note that it was Emmy Noether who first had the idea of such a construction. At the same time she noticed how simple and transparent the proof of the Euler-Poincaré formula becomes if one makes systematic use of the concept of a Betti group. Her remarks in this connection inspired Hopf completely to rework his original proof of the well-known fixed point formula, discovered by Lefschetz in the case of manifolds and generalized by Hopf to the case of arbitrary polyhedra. Hopf's work

"Eine Verallgemeinerung der Euler-Poincaréschen Formel," published in *Göttinger Nachrichten* in 1928, bears the imprint of these remarks of Emmy Noether.

Emmy Noether spent the winter of 1928–1929 in Moscow. She gave a course on abstract algebra at Moscow University and led a seminar on algebraic geometry in the Communist Academy. She quickly established contact with the majority of Moscow mathematicians, in particular, with L. S. Pontryagin and O. Yu. Schmidt. It is not hard to follow the influence of Emmy Noether on the developing mathematical talent of Pontryagin; the strong algebraic flavor in Pontryagin's work undoubtedly profited greatly from his association with Emmy Noether. In Moscow Emmy Noether readily familiarized herself with our life, both scientific and day-to-day. She lived in a modest room in the KSU dormitory near the Krymskii Bridge, and usually walked to the University. She was very interested in the life of our country, especially the life of Soviet youth and the students.

That winter of 1928–1929 I made frequent trips to Smolensk, where I gave lectures on algebra at the Pedagogical Institute. Inspired by continual conversations with Emmy Noether, that year I gave my lectures in her field. Among my listeners A. G. Kurosh immediately stood out; the theories I was presenting, which were imbued with the ideas of Emmy Noether, appealed to his spirit. In this way, through my teaching, Emmy Noether acquired another student, who has since, as we all know, grown into an independent scientist, whose work is still largely concerned with the circle of ideas created by Emmy Noether.

In the spring of 1929 she left Moscow for Göttingen with the firm intention of paying us a return visit within the next few years. Several times she came close to realizing this intention, especially in the last year of her life. After her exile from Germany, she seriously considered finally settling in Moscow, and I had a correspondence with her on this question. She clearly understood that nowhere else were there such possibilities of creating a brilliant new mathematical school to replace the one that was taken from her in Göttingen. And I had already been negotiating with Narkompros about appointing her to a chair in algebra at Moscow University. But, as it happens, Narkompros delayed in making the decision and did not give me a final answer. Meanwhile time was passing, and Emmy Noether, deprived even of the modest salary which she had had in Göttingen, could not wait, and had to accept the invitation from the women's college in the American town of Bryn Mawr.

In Memory, by P. S. Alexandrov

WITH THE DEATH of Emmy Noether I lost the acquaintance of one of the most captivating human beings I have ever known. Her extraordinary kindness of heart, alien to any affectation or insincerity; her cheerfulness and simplicity; her ability to ignore everything that was unimportant in life—created around her an atmosphere of warmth, peace and good will which could never be forgotten by those who associated with her. But her kindness and gentleness never made her weak or unable to resist evil. She had her opinions and was able to advance them with great force and persistence. Though mild and forgiving, her nature was also passionate, temperamental, and strong-willed; she always stated her opinions forthrightly, and did not fear objections. It was moving to see her love for her students, who comprised the basic milieu in which she lived and replaced the family she did not have. Her concern for her students' needs, both scientific and worldly, her sensitivity and responsiveness, were rare qualities. Her great sense of humor, which made both her public appearances and informal association with her especially pleasant, enabled her to deal lightly and without ill will with all of the injustices and absurdities which befell her in her academic career. Instead of taking offense in these situations, she laughed. But she took extreme offense and sharply protested whenever the least injustice was done to one of her students. The entire reservoir of her maternal feelings went to them!

Sociable, good-willed and simple in relations with others, she was able to combine expansiveness with a certain calmness and the absence of any vanity. Glory-seeking and the pursuit of worldly success were alien to her. But she knew her worth, and fought for scientific influence.

In her house—more precisely, in the mansard-roofed apartment she occupied in Göttingen (Friedländerweg 57)—a large group would get together eagerly and often. People of diverse scholarly reputations and positions—from Hilbert, Landau, Brauer and Weyl to the youngest students—would gather at her home and feel relaxed and unconstrained, as in few other scientific salons in Europe. These "festive evenings" in her apartment were arranged on any possible occasion; for example, in the summer of 1927 it was the frequent visits of her student van der Waerden from Holland. The evenings at Emmy Noether's, and the walks with her outside town, were a shining and unforgettable feature of the mathematical life of Göttingen for an entire decade (1923–1932). Many lively mathematical conversations were held during these evenings, but there was also much gaiety and laughter, good

Rhine wine would sometimes be on the table and many sweets would be consumed . . .

Such was Emmy Noether, the greatest of women mathematicians, a leading scientist, wonderful teacher and unforgettable person. She did not have the characteristics of the so-called "woman scholar" or "blue stocking." To be sure, Weyl said in his obituary, "No one could contend that the Graces had stood by her cradle," and he is right, if we have in mind her well-known heavy build. But at this point Weyl is speaking of her not only as a major scientist, but as a major woman! And this she was—her feminine psyche came through in the gentle and delicate lyricism that lay at the foundation of the wide-ranging but never superficial relationships connecting her with people, with her avocation, with the interests of all mankind. She loved people, science, life with all the warmth, all the joy, all the selflessness and all the tenderness of which a deeply feeling heart—and a woman's heart—was capable.

Appendix A

Publications (based on the list added to the obituary by B. L. van der Waerden)
This list does not include papers which were only edited by Emmy Noether.

1. Über die Bildung des Formensystems der ternären biquadratischen Form.
   Sitz. Ber. d. Physikal.-mediz. Sozietät in Erlangen 39 (1907), pp. 176–179.

2. Über die Bildung des Formensystems der ternären biquadratischen Form.
   Journal f. d. reine u. angew. Math. 134 (1908), pp. 23–90.

3. Zur Invariantentheorie der Formen von n Variabeln.
   J. Ber. d. DMV 19 (1910), pp. 101–104.

4. Zur Invariantentheorie der Formen von n Variabeln.
   Journal f. d. reine u. angew. Math. 139 (1911), pp. 118–154.

5. Rationale Funktionenkörper.
   J. Ber. d. DMV 22 (1913), pp. 316–319.

6. Körper und Systeme rationaler Funktionen.
   Math. Ann. 76 (1915), pp. 161–196.

7. Der Endlichkeitssatz der Invarianten endlicher Gruppen.
   Math. Ann. 77 (1916), pp. 89–92.

8. Über ganze rationale Darstellung der Invarianten eines Systems von beliebig vielen Grundformen.
   Math. Ann. 77 (1916), pp. 93–102. (cf. No. 16)

9. Die allgemeinsten Bereiche aus ganzen
   transzendenten Zahlen.
   Math. Ann. 77 (1916), pp. 103–128. (cf. No. 16)

10. Die Funktionalgleichungen der isomorphen
    Abbildung.
    Math. Ann. 77 (1916), pp. 536–545.

11. Gleichungen mit vorgeschriebener Gruppe.
    Math. Ann. 78 (1918), pp. 221–229. (cf. No. 16)

12. Invarianten beliebiger Differentialausdrücke.
    Nachr. v. d. Ges. d. Wiss. zu Göttingen 1918,
    pp. 37–44.

13. Invariante Variationsprobleme.
    Nachr. v. d. Ges. d. Wiss. zu Göttingen 1918,
    pp. 235–257.

14. Die arithmetische Theorie der algebraischen
    Funktionen einer Veränderlichen in ihrer Beziehung
    zu den übrigen Theorien und zu der
    Zahlkörpertheorie.
    J. Ber. d. DMV 28 (1919), pp. 182–203.

15. Die Endlichkeit des Systems der ganzzahligen
    Invarianten binärer Formen.
    Nachr. v. d. Ges. d. Wiss. zu Göttingen 1919,
    pp. 138–156.

16. Zur Reihenentwicklung in der Formentheorie.
    Math. Ann. 81 (1920), pp. 25–30.

17. Moduln in nichtkommutativen Bereichen,
    insbesondere aus Differential- und Differenzenaus-
    drücken. Co-authored by W. Schmeidler. Math.
    Zs. 8 (1920), pp. 1–35.

18. Über eine Arbeit des im Kriege gefallenen K. Hentzelt
    zur Eliminationstheorie.
    J. Ber. d. DMV 30 (1921), p. 101.

19. Idealtheorie in Ringbereichen.
    Math. Ann. 83 (1921), pp. 24–66.

20. Ein algebraisches Kriterium für absolute
    Irreduzibilität.
    Math. Ann. 85 (1922), pp. 26–33.

List of Publications

21. Formale Variationsrechnung und
    Differentialinvarianten.
    Encyklopädie d. math. Wiss. III, 3 (1922), pp. 68–71
    (in: R. Weitzenböck, Differentialinvarianten).

22. Bearbeitung von K. Hentzelt†: Zur Theorie der
    Polynomideale und Resultanten.
    Math. Ann. 88 (1923), pp. 53–79.

23. Algebraische und Differentialvarianten.
    J. Ber. d. DMV 32 (1923), pp. 177–184.

24. Eliminationstheorie und allgemeine Idealtheorie.
    Math. Ann. 90 (1923), pp. 229–261.

25. Eliminationstheorie und Idealtheorie.
    J. Ber. d. DMV 33 (1924), pp. 116–120.

26. Abstrakter Aufbau der Idealtheorie im algebraischen
    Zahlkörper.
    J. Ber. d. DMV 33 (1924), p. 102.

27. Hilbertsche Anzahlen in der Idealtheorie.
    J. Ber. d. DMV 34 (1925), p. 101.

28. Gruppencharaktere und Idealtheorie.
    J. Ber. d. DMV 34 (1925), p. 144.

29. Der Endlichkeitssatz der Invarianten endlicher
    linearer Gruppen der Charakteristik p.
    Nachr. v. d. Ges. d. Wiss. zu Göttingen 1926,
    pp. 28–35.

30. Abstrakter Aufbau der Idealtheorie in algebraischen
    Zahl- und Funktionenkörpern.
    Math. Ann. 96 (1927), pp. 26–61.

31. Der Diskriminantensatz für die Ordnungen eines
    algebraischen Zahl- oder Funktionenkörpers.
    Journal f. d. reine u. angew. Math. 157 (1927),
    pp. 82–104.

32. Über minimale Zerfällungskörper irreduzibler Darstel-
    lungen. Co-authored by R. Brauer. Sitz. Ber. d. Preuß.
    Akad. d. Wiss. 1927, pp. 221–228

33. Hyperkomplexe Größen und Darstellungstheorie in
    arithmetischer Auffassung.
    Atti Congresso Bologna 2 (1928), pp. 71–73.

List of Publications

34. Hyperkomplexe Größen und Darstellungstheorie.
Math. Zs. 30 (1929), pp. 641–692.

35. Über Maximalbereiche aus ganzzahligen Funktionen.
Rec. Soc. Math. Moscou 36 (1929), pp. 65–72.

36. Idealdifferentiation und Differente.
J. Ber. d. DMV 39 (1930), p. 17.

37. Normalbasis bei Körpern ohne höhere Verzweigung.
Journal f. d. reine u. angew. Math. 167 (1932), pp. 147–152.

38. Beweis eines Hauptsatzes in der Theorie der Algebren.
Co-authored by R. Brauer and H. Hasse. Journal f. d. reine u. angew. Math. 167 (1932), pp. 399–404.

39. Hyperkomplexe Systeme in ihren Beziehungen zur kommutativen Algebra und zur Zahlentheorie.
Verhandl. Intern. Math.-Kongreß Zürich 1 (1932), pp. 189–194.

40. Nichtkommutative Algebren.
Math. Zs. 37 (1933), pp. 514–541.

41. Der Hauptgeschlechtssatz für relativ-galoissche Zahlkörper.
Math. Ann. 108 (1933), pp. 411–419.

42. Zerfallende verschränkte Produkte und ihre Maximalordnungen.
Actualités scientifiques et industrielles 148 (1934) (15 pages).

43. Idealdifferentiation und Differente.
Journal f. d. reine u. angew. Math. 188 (1950), pp. 1–21.

Doctoral Dissertations Completed under Emmy Noether
The first date indicates the day on which the degree was granted, and the second the date and place of publication.

Falckenberg, Hans, Dec. 16, 1911, Erlangen
Verzweigungen von Lösungen nichtlinearer
Differentialgleichungen   Leipzig 1912

List of Publications

Seidelmann, Fritz, March 4, 1916, Erlangen
Die Gesamtheit der kubischen und
biquadratischen Gleichungen mit Affekt bei
beliebigem Rationalitätsbereich   Erlangen 1916

Hermann, Grete, Feb. 25, 1925, Göttingen
Die Frage der endlich vielen Schritte in der
Theorie der Polynomideale unter Benutzung
nachgelassener Sätze von Kurt Hentzelt   Berlin 1926

Grell, Heinrich, July 14, 1926, Göttingen
Beziehungen zwischen den Idealen
verschiedener Ringe   Berlin 1927

Hölzer, Rudolf, died before the degree was
granted.
Zur Theorie der primären Ringe   Berlin 1927

Weber, Werner, June 12, 1929, Göttingen
Idealtheoretische Deutung der
Darstellbarkeit beliebiger natürlicher Zahlen
durch quadratische Formen   Berlin 1930

Levitzki, Jakob, June 26, 1929, Göttingen
Über vollständig reduzible Ringe und
Unterringe   Berlin 1931

Deuring, Max, June 18, 1930, Göttingen
Zur arithmetischen Theorie der algebraischen
Funktionen   Berlin 1932

Fitting, Hans, July 29, 1931, Göttingen
Zur Theorie der Automorphismenringe
Abelscher Gruppen und ihr Analogon bei
nichtkommutativen Gruppen   Berlin 1933

Witt, Ernst, July 27, 1933, Göttingen
Riemann-Rochscher Satz und Zeta-Funktion
im Hyperkomplexen   Berlin 1934

Tsen, Chiungtze, Dec. 6, 1933, Göttingen
Algebren über Funktionenkörpern   Göttingen
1934

Schilling, Otto, 1934, Marburg
Über gewisse Beziehungen zwischen der
Arithmetik hyperkomplexer Zahlsysteme
und algebraischer Zahlkörper   Braunschweig
1935

Stauffer, Ruth, 1935, Bryn Mawr
The construction of a normal basis in a
separable extension field   Baltimore
                                             1936

Appendix B

Obituaries of Emmy Noether

1. The *New York Herald Tribune*, April 15, 1935, p. 12.
2. A. Einstein, Princeton, N.J.; The *New York Times*, May 4, 1935, p. 12 (letters to the editor).
3. J. Barinaga, Madrid; *Revista Matematica Hispano-Americana* 1935, pp. 162–163.
4. B. L. van der Waerden, Leipzig; *Mathematische Annalen* 111, 1935, pp. 469–476.
5. A. Sagastume Berra, La Plata; *Publicaciones de la Facultad de ciencias físico-matématicas de la Universidad nacional de La Plata* 104, 1935, pp. 95–96.
6. H. Weyl, Princeton, N.J.; *Scripta mathematica* III, 3, 1935, pp. 201–220, including a portrait.*
7. V. Kořinek, Prague; *Časopis pro pěstovárí matematiky a fysiky* 65, 1935, section D, pp. 1–6.
8. P. S. Alexandrov, Moscow, memorial address delivered before the Mathematical Society of Moscow, September 5, 1935.

* This obituary is reproduced, verbatim, in English, in *Gesammelte Abhandlungen von Hermann Weyl*, published by Springer in 1968; also in this book, pp. 112–152.

Appendix C

List of Academic Ranks and Terms
(*with English equivalent or explanation*)

Assistent, assistant professor

ausserordentlicher Universitätsprofessor, a professor with somewhat limited internal administrative rights and functions

Dozent, lecturer

Habilitation, Habilitierung, the act of receiving the official right to teach at a given university, or 'venia legendi'

Habilitierungsakt, file connected with the process of achieving 'venia legendi'

Hospitant, student teacher

nichtbeamteter ausserordentlicher Professor mit Lehrauftrag, a. o. professor, see above, without tenure but with a teaching assignment.

ordentlicher Lehrstuhl, position of full professor, chair

ordentlicher Professor (see Ordinarius)

Ordinarius, full professor

Privatdozent, in those days, an unpaid lecturer with 'venia legendi' (right to teach)

Realgymnasium, high school leading to university with emphasis on science, mathematics and modern languages

Reifeprüfung, graduation from high school, usually at age 19, admitting the student to a university of his choice

Untertertia, eighth grade

Index

Index

192